MILLIONAIRE MAKER MANUAL

By
ANDY ALBRIGHT

ISBN: 978-0-9846501-2-5

Manufactured in the United States of America

Book Design by Rebecca Paskins
Cover Design by Barry Stephenson and Rebecca Paskins
Illustrations by Rebecca Paskins

CONTENTS

RAW MATERIALS   79

OUR SYSTEM 139

DEDICATION

I dedicated my first book, *The 8 Steps to Success*, to my wife Jane, so I only saw it fitting to dedicate my second book, *Millionaire Maker Manual*, to my children—Haleigh (17) and Spencer (14).

 I felt it appropriate to dedicate this "how to" book to them because I am consistent in explaining to them "how to" stand tall among the crowd and not follow the masses, but rather turn and go in the opposite direction. As a father and mentor, I have taught them that  working hard, helping people, and having an overall vision without blinders does result in dreams becoming realities.

My desire for them both is that through witnessing the heart I have for helping others and truly making a difference that they, in turn, one day will also long to serve, give, and love unconditionally.

With this, I dedicate this second book to you, Haleigh Jane Albright and Spencer Crawford Albright—for all the years you cheered me on to "stay true to the course" and build a dynasty—I say thank you. Your love, support, and smiles are what kept me in the hunt.

I love you!
Daddy

A NOTE FROM THE AUTHOR

TO THE READERS OF THIS MANUAL:

I feel honored that you have chosen the *Millionaire Maker Manual* to read. The techniques given within have worked for me and many others because it is the attention to the tiniest detail that makes the biggest difference. It is with a true desire that I hope you will find the manual useful. It is my belief and faith in God that has helped me overcome to become.

> *"I can do all things through Christ who strengthens me."*
>
> **–Philippians 4:13**

May you find a nugget or two within the pages that will encourage you to "move" from where you are and become a leading example for others to follow.

I sincerely thank my God, my family, and my business associates for always believing in me and supporting me. Because of you I stand proud, I hold fast to my beliefs, and I love having fun, making money, and making a difference.

–Andy Albright

DISCLAIMER

This manual is meant for internal use only and is not for public circulation. In no way should any part of this book be reproduced in any shape, form, or manner. It should only be used within the company for the purpose of educating and training.

No statement, graph, illustration, or statistic in *Millionaire Maker Manual*, shall be used as any type of contractual agreement, nor will it modify or serve as a supplement to any existing contractual agreements between the company, the author, or any member of the company.

The content of this book, which deals with recruiting others to join our organization, can affect commissions of agents; therefore, the information contained within should not be used to gauge past or projected future earnings of agents.

Millionaire Maker Manual is only intended to serve as a guide to help agents through the process of building a sales team. Only licensed agents should speak about products and services offered. All sales are made based on the needs, product sensibility, and financial affordability of the clients.

The strategies presented are based on 10 years of trial-and-error approaches. The information given is based on what typically has worked and what has not. Potential prospects are not required to purchase any products or services of any kind with the intention of becoming an agent.

Despite seeing numerous licensed agents experience highly successful careers using this system; Millionaire Maker Manual is based on individual cases. A number of variables can impact results and income levels: work ethic, work patterns, dedication, persistence, activity levels, and many other factors. All participants achieve different levels, and these levels often change over time. An agent's true results cannot be predicted even when he/she is following the information contained in *Millionaire Maker Manual*.

The publisher and author will take no responsibility or liability to any person or entity with respect to any losses or damages caused, or alleged to have been caused—directly or indirectly—by the contents of this book. *Millionaire Maker Manual* is sold with the understanding that neither the publisher, nor the author is giving legal, accounting, or any other professional services or advice.

The views, thoughts, opinions, and information written in *Millionaire Maker Manual* are those of the author and do not necessarily express the views and opinions of any other person or the company represented.

FOREWORD

BY TIM GOAD (FOUNDER, TIM GOAD INTERNATIONAL)

When I first met Andy Albright 20 years ago, I had no idea that we would be where we are today. We've traveled together all across this great country, and during those travels I have been fortunate to witness explosive growth in Andy, both professionally and personally. He continues to be a loving husband and father, a leader who moves people to greater heights, and a man who continually strives to help people get the most out of life—theirs.

This book, Andy's second in roughly a year, is about his strategy to build an effective sales organization. With National Agents Alliance, Andy now has a powerful vehicle to accomplish great things. What sets Andy apart is his servant's heart, his willingness to share that which has been granted to him, to drive the NAA vehicle to do great, positive deeds that impact not only his life and his family's life, but also the lives of all those he touches.

Rarely in history is there an individual like Andy, who has a vision so big it affects the lives of thousands and thousands of people he will never even meet, but NAA does just that. Clients from coast-to-coast, agents in every state, and all the home office staff enjoy a better life today because Andy took action on an idea. Andy's action and burning desire transformed a BIG, GREAT idea into a reality.

Andy doesn't just talk the talk, he walks the walk. He is relentless in his determination to "make a difference" in people's lives, and he continues to build NAA into a close-knit team, based on sound training, with a "One Band, One Sound" level of togetherness. His sense of family carries over to all his relationships, and that trait is rare indeed in corporate America.

Through his ability to be a great family man, a phenomenal friend, and a superior leader, Andy inspires the confidence and loyalty that is taking National Agents Alliance to the very top of the insurance industry. Andy's ideas have helped thousands of families, of agents and clients alike, live their lives worry free, every day, every night, now and forever.

I am honored to call Andy Albright my friend and my brother. I am thankful for our shared vision to make a difference and make it BIG! I love you, Andy! Keep dreaming big dreams and keep reaching for the stars. I cannot wait to see how the journey unfolds.

–Tim Goad

TIM GOAD INTERNATIONAL
52 Riley Road #219
Celebration, Florida 34747
www.TimGoad.com

INTRODUCTION

It's the fall of 2011, and I'm thrilled to be working in an industry that not only changed my life, but has already affected thousands of people. It's made a world of difference for my family. Our income has grown to proportions that I never anticipated.

In November of 2010, I took sole leadership of the company and the title of President and Chief Executive Officer. I hired consultants that have been extremely successful in other companies and industries. I partnered with people like Jim Henson, Barry Clarkson, Tim Goad, Derek Steed, John Roberts, and Harry Stout.

JIM HENSON

Jim Henson joined us in a consulting role in November of 2008. Since then, he has helped NAA diversify, by adding products and carriers the company didn't have previously. Henson's 35-plus years of experience in the insurance industry make him a valuable consultant to NAA, where he serves as Chief Operations Consultant. Again, his strong suit for us is in dealing with product development and design, product implementation, marketing packages, and long-term marketing strategies and direction.

Jim Henson speaking in April 2011 on the SilverSea Cruise, sponsored by Foresters.

Henson's a Master Yoda-like figure to us because he has seen and pretty much done everything related to the industry of insurance sales. Having a man with his experience and knowledge involved with us is invaluable when you hit roadblocks. His experience in the last 35-plus years serving as President and Chief Marketing Officer for several insurance companies, including Occidental Life of North Carolina, Integon Life Insurance Corporation, Georgia International Life Insurance Company, and Pennisular Life Insurance Company prove to be an asset. He began his career as an agent in 1970 and worked his way up through various management and officer levels. Prior to joining NAA, Henson worked as Senior Vice-President and Chief Marketing Officer for Shenandoah Life Insurance Company. During his 10-year tenure there, he increased agent distribution from just more than 500 agents to more than 13,000 active agents. Sales also jumped more than 2,000 percent, from $11 million to more than $200 million per year, and assets almost tripled in that time. NAA is fortunate to have Henson serving as a valuable member of the corporate team.

BARRY CLARKSON

Barry Clarkson serves as a consultant and mentor to NAA agents. AKA Mr. NAActivity.

Barry Clarkson's personal success in the insurance industry lends itself to serve as an advocate as well as a consultant for Andy and the entire NAA team. Clarkson's expertise and belief in the fact that proper "activity yields results" plays an active role in the guidance that he offers to the team. His wealth of knowledge and his heart for helping others succeed prove over and over what an asset he is to others. Clarkson's "polished" demeanor, his ability to gage success, and his belief in others certainly makes him a valuable member of our organization.

TIM GOAD

I first met Tim Goad 20 years ago through my involvement with another company. Tim's strengths are numerous. His involvement with ministry, music, speaking, and leadership development for more than 30 years has proven to be a true asset to the company. Tim, his wife Gaye, and their children—Blake and BreAnn—are involved in multiple organizations that help provide food, shelter, clothing, and medicine to the needy worldwide. Tim brings a "culture" to the organization by

Tim Goad having fun while speaking to our agents at NAA's 2011 National Convention in Raleigh, NC

sharing his wealth of knowledge on relationships, teamwork, and leadership.

As Chief Cultural Consultant, Tim's role is to serve as a mentor to our corporate staff as well as the NAA agent force. Tim's vision of "making a difference" echoes the philosophy of NAA and his ability to share this vision creates an environment where success breeds.

DEREK STEED

Derek Steed, a highly-respected attorney in N.C., serves as outside general counsel for NAA.

Derek Steed's list of accomplishments, community involvement, and accolades are far too many to list here. He's a phenomenal attorney/partner with Wishart, Norris, Henninger and Pittman in Burlington, North Carolina. He serves as general counsel for NAA and confirms that NAA is compliant in the industry and conducts business properly. Derek's superior guidance is truly an asset to the NAA team.

JOHN ROBERTS

John Roberts during a Manager's Meeting at NAA's 2011 National Convention in Raleigh, NC.

John Roberts, a partner-in-charge of insurance services for Dixon Hughes Goodman (High Point, North Carolina office), has 10 years of public accounting experience. During his career, he has concentrated in the insurance industry, specifically in life insurance. With NAA, Roberts serves as a liaison and a voice for accounting issues that impact our organizational and financial success.

HARRY STOUT

Harry Stout has more than 30 years of experience in the areas of accounting, insurance, and financial services. He has served as Chief Executive Officer of Australian operations for ING. His background with Old Mutual Life Holdings (President and CEO),

Harry Stout is a veteran of the insurance industry and has held key positions with ING, Old Mutual, and F&G.

other Fidelity and Guaranty Life companies, and United Pacific Life has led to his strong knowledge of annuity and insurance products, services, and markets. His library of personal knowledge and experiences adds much value to the NAA team as a whole.

Also, I started listening and hearing my wife Jane more than I had previously. She has a master's degree in education, was a teacher for eight years, and has survived building several businesses with me, which is one of her biggest accomplishments. She has been there when things were not all that great, and she's stuck by me each

My wife and my friend Jane, who has stuck by me throughout our journey.

time I've had a crazy idea. Jane's biggest accomplishment is raising our children—Haleigh (17) and Spencer (14). They are great kids, and part of that is due to Jane being such a devoted mother.

I also looked internally and realized that getting "back to the basics" was something that I needed to do to impact thousands and thousands of people. I realized that I never should have strayed from those basics and decided that we would spend more time focusing on getting back to those basics.

My first book, *The 8 Steps to Success*, was released in June of 2010. Thousands of copies were sold, and it made such an impact on the people associated with National Agents Alliance that I decided a systematic, manual-style book, a library of resources was needed to help people understand the basics of how to put this business together.

I started a blog (www.AndyAlbright.com) that many people read. The feedback generated by the blog was influential in the decision to write this book.

Tim Goad encouraged me in many different ways to document and simplify a system of how to create what I create. I also read the book, *Switch*, by Chip and Dan Heath, which made me think in simpler and more basic ways. One of my favorite companies is Keller-Williams Realty, and they have a great teaching book, *The M.R.E. Agent*, that explains their system in great detail.

I wanted NAA to have a manual to teach the basics in great detail. Thus, *Millionaire Maker Manual* was birthed.

If a system is worked properly, the system will often work. "If you work it, it will work!" Documenting the system is a daunting task. It almost seems impossible.

What I realized as our business started to explode in the summer of 2011 is that we focused more on the system rather than on all the "rah rah" stuff.

The idea was to have our key team members focus intently on the building of NAA as a whole and not just their individual teams that are a part of the NAA entity.

The objective here was to remove the feeling of being the "Lone Ranger" and to confirm that there is no "I" in team. TEAM: "Together Everyone Achieves More" took life!

My friend John C. Maxwell writes in the book, *The 21 Irrefutable Laws of Leadership*, in Chapter 16 titled "The Law of the Big Mo," that momentum can and will cover a multitude of errors.

"Why do I say that momentum really is a leader's best friend?" Maxwell wrote. "Because many times it's the only thing that makes the difference between losing and winning. When you have no momentum, even the simplest tasks seem impossible."

We know that we are going to make errors, but as we get together and create momentum we will overcome each other's weaknesses. We now continue to simplify and unify our strategies. In fact, it is not good enough to tell people to keep it simple; we are providing them the necessary tools to help them KEEP IT SIMPLE.

With that in mind, *Millionaire Maker Manual* was written with incredible fury and intensity. There's no doubt there will be updated editions in the future, because it's like anything else. Over time, everything changes. As we uncover more solutions, we will continue to improve and implement better, simplified instructions, so look for more to come in the future. It is a process.

Our belief in building people and our confidence in this industry has never been stronger. Never!

We know we can work together and utilize the system. We can duplicate, systemize, and syndicate a system such that anybody can overcome weaknesses and produce success on a repeated, clock-like basis. With the correct degree of discipline and with the correct degree of desire, we can change not only our own lives and our children's lives, but also our grandchildren, our great grandchildren, and so on! Basically, this is a legacy in the making, which will affect future generations to come.

World, watch out! We are on the grow!

THE
FACTORY

"How would you act if you knew beyond a shadow of a doubt that you would win if you followed these directions? How would you proceed? How would you invest? How would you focus? How would you deal with the following pages? If you knew beyond a shadow of a doubt in your subconscious mind that there was no way in the world that you would lose, that you were guaranteed to succeed, how would you proceed?"

–Andy Albright

DUPLICATION EXPLANATION

Most businesses fail. That's a negative way to start talking to budding entrepreneurs; however, that has been a fact in American business. Reasons for these failures include lack of duplication, lack of a proven method, lack of a mentor, lack of a recipe, lack of a plan, lack of capital, lack of a market, lack of a goal, and lack of an overall system!

There are also a large number of businesses that don't fail, and some great examples of those are Krispy Kreme, McDonald's, Subway, and Domino's.

A lot of people say it began when Ray Kroc started McDonald's because he understood how to create something so simple that anybody could operate it and succeed. I love when you walk into a McDonald's and place your order; and then the employee asks if you would like to "super size" that? It's like they have signs up everywhere blinking that everybody has to say the same thing. Their directions are simple, and they are clear.

MCDONALD'S

Kroc was a high school dropout-turned-businessman, who took over the small-scale McDonald's Corporation franchise in 1954 and built it into the most successful fast-food chain in the world. He created a fortune during his lifetime, ended up owning Major League Baseball's San Diego Padres, and was named one of *Time* magazine's Most Important People of the Century. Kroc was a Prince Castle multi-mixer (milkshake) machine salesman early in his career and sold eight units to the McDonald brothers for some of their restaurants. He eventually bought the McDonald brothers' restaurants and pushed to open more stores across the United States. He maintained the "Speedee Service System" assembly line for hamburger production that the McDonald brothers implemented in 1948. He standardized operations in an effort to make sure that whether you were in New York, Dallas or Chicago, every single "Big Mac" burger would taste the same with "two all-beef patties, special sauce, lettuce, cheese, pickles, onions on a sesame-seed bun." He set strict rules for franchises on how the food would be made, the portion sizes, the cooking methods and times, and the packaging of food. Kroc rejected cost-cutting measures like using soybean hamburger patties. His rules also applied to customer service standards, which mandated that money be refunded for orders not filled within five minutes. Kroc took the McDonald brothers' system, tweaked it in spots, and made it an even more efficient system, a system that was so successful it allowed him to live—and enjoy—an amazing life.

SUBWAY

In an effort to raise money for college, Fred DeLuca, then 17 years old, borrowed $1,000 from a family friend—Peter Buck—to start his first sandwich shop in August of 1965. Since then, a little store we call Subway has popped up all over the world and consistently ranks among *Entrepreneur* magazine's Franchise 500 rankings. At the end of 2010, Subway had surpassed McDonald's with 33,749 restaurants worldwide. That number has since climbed to right at 35,000 stores in 98 countries and territories. That's a lot of $5 foot-long subs!

Do you think DeLuca and Buck, who has a Ph.D., thought their outfit would grow to those levels when they started? Probably not, but they did keep trying to grow, and eventually had multiple stores across the United States. They were too busy working on getting bigger and better to worry about where they would be in 2011. They were smart enough to keep working because they understood that "if you work it, it will work!" That's the mindset we want our people to have every day.

KRISPY KREME

In 1933, Krispy Kreme's founder Vernon Rudolph purchased a doughnut shop in Kentucky along with a "secret" recipe for yeast-raised doughnuts. After selling the doughnuts locally for a while, Rudolph moved operations to Nashville, Tennessee in order to meet customer demand. He sold his interest in that company in 1937 and moved to Winston-Salem, North Carolina, where Krispy Kreme was born. Rudolph started selling to grocery stores and eventually sold directly to customers. Krispy Kreme was growing, and by the 1960s it was known throughout the southeast. Now, it's known in places all over the world and is publicly traded on the New York Stock Exchange under the symbol KKD. Mr. Rudolph probably never imagined how big his little local doughnut shop would be one day. He had a system, and it worked out well for him! "Hot Now" neon signs are recognized throughout the doughnut lover's world and you want to get 'em while they're hot.

DOMINO'S

On June 10th of 1960, brothers Tom and James Monaghan borrowed $500 and made a $75 down payment to take over Dominick's Pizza, a small pizzeria in Michigan. Dominick's quickly became Domino's, and Tom bought out his brother by giving him a second-hand car. By the late 1970s, there were more than 200 Domino's franchises in the United States. Domino's Pizza then went international in 1983.

What is amazing is that for the longest time Domino's was resistant to any changes. Tom Monaghan was stubborn when it came to his little pizza shop. The menu, for instance, was simple and streamlined. Customers had the choice of one type of crust, which was named the regular pizza, so you could order the "regular" or the "regular." You did have a choice of a small or large pizza. Domino's offered pizza and Coke for the longest time and it worked, but Pizza Hut, Papa John's, and Little Caesars forced Domino's to change things up.

After being in business for more than 30 years, Domino's unveiled its "Deep Pan" pizza in 1989. This was a reaction to all other competitors rolling out new, exciting pizzas. The move solidified the company, and Domino's opened its 5,000th store later that year.

In 1992, Domino's first non-pizza item, the bread stick, was introduced. A little reluctant to offer a "non-pizza" item, Domino's offered a pizza dipping sauce for the bread sticks—a very popular move that increased sales.

In 1994, Domino's went to the barn yard and introduced chicken wings to its menu. By 1996, the company had reached global levels —even adding stores in Egypt and other locations—and sales flirted with the $3 billion mark.

While they did resist change for about 40 years, Domino's is still viewed as an industry innovator. The belt-driven pizza oven was a Domino's invention; they were one of the first to use corrugated cardboard delivery boxes to help retain the heat of a pizza pie until it reached your home, and they developed the "Heat Wave," a portable electrical bag system drivers used to keep your pizza warm during delivery.

The changes Domino's made were for two reasons: to help the company become better and to keep customers happy and coming back. Domino's did this by becoming more efficient and by producing a higher quality product.

Tom Monaghan retired in 1998 and sold 93 percent of Domino's for $1 billion dollars. Not a million, but a BILLION dollars. Not a bad return on his $500 investment.

A 2009 consumer taste preference survey conducted by Brand Keys delivered news that Domino's did not want to hear. Domino's tied for dead last with Chuck E. Cheese's for the worst-tasting pizza. The company didn't waste any time. It began a campaign to improve quality, and the chefs were shown trying to improve the product in television commercials. Within a year, a new pizza was introduced, Domino's celebrated its 50th year in business (2010), and J. Patrick Doyle was named as its new CEO. The improvements resulted in a 14.3 percent boost in quarterly profits, one of the biggest quarterly jumps by a major fast-food chain ever recorded. By changing its pizza recipe "from the crust up," Domino's reconnected with customers it had lost over the years to places like Pizza Hut, Papa John's, and Little Caesars. Domino's new recipe worked because they listened to the customer and made improvements where it made sense to do so.

If you know something is wrong and you don't fix it, then you are going to continue to have problems. As Albert Einstein said, "insanity is doing the same thing, over and over, and expecting different results." You can't be afraid to make changes, especially when you know they are needed.

> *"Insanity is doing the same thing, over and over, and expecting different results."*
>
> *–Albert Einstein*

Kroc, Monaghan, DeLuca, and Rudolph were all pioneers in business who proved the value of a duplicating system. A major purpose of this book is to teach the NAA success system that will allow you to build a duplicating business with no limits on what you can accomplish. Follow in the footsteps of these great businessmen, follow the NAA system, and stay committed to your goals…you can't fail!

In a traditional business you have to learn "stuff," and think ahead to be creative. Franchises that thrive typically use the phrase, "duplicate, don't innovate." It's not that they don't want you to have your own personality, and be your own person, but they also want you to be successful and they have clear-cut instructions in place for you to follow. It's a system of duplication that has worked repeatedly. It has been proven that people who follow this system are successful, and it can work for you too.

It's like a factory. I worked at Bojangles', one of the most successful fast-food chains. They showed me how to cut the biscuit, how to take a piece of ham, put it between the bread, fold the paper over the top and slide it over the little bar for another person to take.

They even told me at what temperature to keep the warming light. Everything was basically simple. I used to laugh so hard because I said anybody can do this, but apparently you have to SHOW UP to do it, and you have to WORK to do it. Those are two things that most people can do. Having a system that is duplicatable keeps it simple. You just have to be willing to work (and many people are not), be willing to learn, and be willing to copy—something I knew I could do with time and energy.

When a person first gets started with NAA, they want to know what to do. I want to refer to the old 1967 Oscar-winning movie *Cool Hand Luke*, which was directed by Stuart Rosenberg. We love to joke about how the sheriff tells Luke to "get his mind right."

When people join our organization, they come from incredibly different backgrounds. Some people have money in the bank, some are ridiculously broke, some are college educated, some have a GED, some have business backgrounds, and some have no business knowledge at all. We have young adults—as young as 18 or 19—and we have older people, some in their 60s and 70s that join us as well. There is much to learn—you, therefore, need to get your "mind right." Anytime you start a business you start thinking about things like do I need office space? Do I need to hire and train employees? Do I pay them on a W-2? What about a 1099 form? How do I learn the tricks of the trade? How do I track my inventory? How do I keep up with my bills? How do I do all these things? What do I do next?

"What do I do next?"

–Anonymous

Let me clearly state this: we cannot produce a miracle overnight. You are going to have to put in some energy, some time, and a lot of effort to become successful with our organization. We have been quoted as saying that "a person who thinks they can do this like we have done it, who thinks they can build large businesses, who thinks they can produce results like we have produced without time, effort, and energy is really arrogant."

We are offended that someone could be so arrogant to think they can build a multi-million dollar business without effort.

What I would ask you to do is to give yourself time and some runway to clear the trees like when a plane takes off. The plane has to have enough room to gather momentum, expend some fuel, and soar high enough to clear the trees. Please give yourself some time and plan to work hard. Understand this: you were brought into this business by somebody that wants to expand their business. They experience success when you are having success. Therefore, you need to understand that you are in business for yourself, but you are not by yourself. We have a system set up that gives you guidance, planning, and step-by-step instruction. We have mentors and growing managers that we REQUIRE to provide the training for you. We have events such as National Convention, Fall Forwards, Spring Forwards, Leadership Conferences, and other various events around the country that we have carefully built, nurtured, and designed to give you all the support you need. Our newest events, known as All-Access Pass and Rotation meetings (see www.NAAHotSpots.com for more information) provide incredible teaching tools and specific training designed for our team.

We say that it takes YOUR WORK to make the DREAM WORK.

However, you will have to use these tools and the system in order for them to become a part of who you are. We say that it takes YOUR WORK to make the DREAM WORK. We ask this: would you rather enjoy the pain of discipline or endure the pain of regret? The pain of regret is like Hell, but the pain of discipline is just a temporary burn.

Yes, if you have a full-time job and this is a second job, career, or business, it does require some adjustments, extra

Would you rather enjoy the pain of discipline or endure the pain of regret?

time, and energy to learn our business. In the Bible, Galatians 6:9 reads, "And let us not grow weary of doing good; for in due season we will reap, if we do not give up."

If you don't give up, and you don't let the roadblocks stop you, you will succeed.

Somebody could laugh at you for trying to actually do something different in your life and become a better person. Your spouse could have a heavy load and this just adds to it. Your children may be looking at you funny because of what you are trying to do. These are emotional issues that you have to deal with and you are going to have to "get your mind right, and I mean right," like the sheriff tells Luke when he twice catches him trying to get out of jail and shackles him with a set of chains each time. The sheriff warns Luke there won't be a third time because he's going to make sure Luke "gets his mind right."

Poor Luke, he never really learned, did he?

How do we stay focused? How do we make it? It's inch by inch. It's step by step. With our system, each inch and each step counts toward the ultimate goal. You must keep that in mind when you start the journey.

As you build your own team, you have to learn to trust your coach and your mentor. We all have to work together because your success at NAA is dependent on team success. There has to be a trust with the leaders of the organization that is developed as we go. Now to be clear, the leaders must live up to this trust. They must respect other parts of the organization and other people in the organization. There is a book written by Stephen Covey Jr. called *The Speed of Trust*. As we've hired people from advertisements, newspapers, and Internet advertising, we've noticed that it takes longer to build trust with them as opposed to hiring a friend's friend through networking. If we can hire a person that trusts us from the start, then we can develop trust with them faster and that relates directly to Covey's book. In his book, he explains that trusts equals confidence while distrust equates to suspicion.

My friend, Dave Anderson, who wrote *How to Build Your Business by the Book*, also says it is better to hire from referrals.

In general, coaches of any team typically talk to the team members in regards to trust. Trust is an important ingredient for effective communication on a team. Trust among team members encourages the team to work together for a common goal. If

Dave Anderson and Andy Albright at NAA's 2011 National Convention in Raleigh, NC.

trust is betrayed within the team, often times the cohesiveness of the team is lost.

Trust is a characteristic that is earned over time and is important in securing relationships.

Covey's book dedicates an entire section focused on trust in relationships. "The truth is that in every relationship—personal and professional—what you do has far greater impact than anything you say," Covey wrote. More often than not, your actions will always speak louder than anything you can say, even if you are the greatest salesman in the world. It's great to say you are going to do something, but the longer you wait to actually do the activity, the less weight your words carry.

It's clear that, if you only talk and never deliver, people will distance themselves from your rhetoric. Your words, coupled with a lack of action, can destroy relationships that took years to grow. If you always deliver then you have nothing

> *"People don't listen to you speak; they watch your feet."*
>
> *–Anonymous*

to worry about. If you deliver consistently, the value of your words will become more valuable and your reputation will remain pure. That's where the trust part comes into play. When this happens, you will be able to ask people to do things and they will be willing to do them because of who you are. They trust you and you can get them to move. The art of getting people to "move" is a powerful tool to have in your arsenal when you are leading a team. People want to trust you, so don't give them any reason not to. This is important in new acquaintances that you recruit to join your team. It's going to be easier for people to trust you if you've never given them reasons not to.

> *"If your dream ain't bigger than you, there's a problem with your dream."*
>
> *– NFL Hall of Famer Deion Sanders*

Dave Anderson writes about the "Dirty Dozen Causes of Management Failure" in *How to Run Your Business by the Book* and the fifth cause he lists is this: "Distrust from employees because of character issues like failing to admit mistakes." Anderson knows breaking someone's trust means they will have no commitment to you. It's really difficult to convince a person to do more when they don't trust you, and if they don't trust you, it's likely that they don't like you either. You are going to be dealing with a person that just "does the minimum" once that trust is broken. Without building trust throughout your organization it will be very difficult to achieve your goals and reach your dreams.

If you have a tiny dream, a tiny problem can stop you. If you have a tiny goal, a tiny problem can stop you. If you have a BIG goal, a tiny problem won't stop you. One of our recommendations is to get a "BHAG," like Jim Collins talks about in his book, Good to Great.

If you want to know what a "BHAG" is ask my buddy Chris Gardner. He told our people at our 2011 Leadership Conference to read his book *The Pursuit of Happyness* if they wanted to know why he wore two watches. I recommend you read *Good to Great* to find out that "BHAG" is:

BIG HAIRY AUDACIOUS GOAL

Collins coined this phrase in an effort to help employees focus on their goals and to work together in a positive manner. "A BHAG is a huge and daunting goal—like a big mountain to climb," Collins writes. "It is clear, compelling and people 'get it' right away. A BHAG serves as a unifying focal point of effort, galvanizing people and creating a team spirit as people strive toward a finish line. Like the 1960s NASA moon mission, A BHAG captures the imagination and grabs people in the gut."

It can be a simple goal like boosting sales or revenue growth 10 percent in six months. It's about a company defining its vision and mission statement, then setting out to reach that goal. Maybe it's a goal that your company sets for 10 to 30 years down the road.

Make your BHAG clear and decisive. It will serve as a unifying focal point of effort in your business. It will serve as a team booster. There is a visible end in sight that everybody knows about. Set a goal and let your people start shooting for it. In the chapter "Good to Great to Built to Last" of *Good to Great*, Collins writes about the difference between good BHAGs and bad BHAGs. A bad BHAG is based on chest-thumping and bravado, while a good BHAG is set with a clear understanding of what you can be, what you should be, and what is driving you in that direction. When you set a good BHAG, it's a mix of core values and purpose.

Good-to-great companies build deeply-rooted, strong, committed management teams. If you can find a core group of people that are committed to helping your business go from good to great, then you are on track. It's all about finding the RIGHT people.

Even with the right people, things are going to happen from time to time. That's why setting your goals correctly and properly is very important. If you don't set the bar high enough, then you won't achieve big goals. Set your goal high enough that even if you come up just short, you are still in a great position.

If you want to create an extra $5,000 a month we suggest that you shoot for $20,000. We know that problems will come up from time to time, and interesting things that we call obstacles do come up. Some people believe overcoming those obstacles makes success that much sweeter. Problems are going to come up no matter what you are in pursuit of—it is life—it happens. For example, if you decided to go to the beach today, which might be three hours away depending on where you are, there will be problems you encounter along the way. There might be road construction, you could get a flat tire, or maybe you experience car trouble. Something could happen, but because you are so excited about where you are going, you are willing to deal with those road blocks in order to get to your desired destination. You are so pumped about being at the beach that you are willing to deal with whatever comes your way to get there. It's worth it to you to go through all that to be on the sand and in the water.

We recommend "going for the gold," reaching for the highest level possible, and making it happen. Believe how wonderful it's going to be when you are on the beach, having conquered the obstacles you faced along your journey. Thinking that way will help get you through some of the little problems you are going to face in the beginning.

Build your duplicating NAA business the right way by following the system. Set some audacious goals. Build strong relationships throughout your team by developing a deep level of trust and commitment. Lead from the front. Be the example to your team— learn from the successful leaders and, then, be that leader.

START RIGHT NOW

GET LICENSED

First of all, you need to sign up to get your life insurance and health insurance license. In every single state there are different scenarios due to differing laws and regulations. We have a licensing department at NAA that you can call to find out EXACTLY what you need to do in order to obtain your license. Check out www.nationalagentsalliance.com/contact-us/ and look for contact information in the contracting and licensing section of the page. You will find phone numbers and e-mail addresses for people who can point you in the right direction.

We have two national contracts; one with ExamFX and the other with WebCE. You can go to the following web sites: www.examfx.com for ExamFX and www.webce.com for WebCE for more information. Both have worked with many of the top insurance companies and financial institutions across the United States to solve their state insurance pre-licensing needs. ExamFX courses are streamlined, saving new candidates time in the study process to get them in the field faster and writing business. In each state they follow the Department of Insurance outline verbatim, meaning no fluff, no funny business, and only the information necessary to pass the state exam the first time.

ExamFX has more than 275,000 associates training with their material nationally. To enroll in one of their interactive online training courses visit the ExamFX URL listed previously, or call 1-800-586-2253 to speak with one of their customer service representatives.

WebCE was founded in 1992 and is the leading supplier of state-of-the-art continuing education courses to licensed insurance professionals and financial planners. WebCE's mission is to "provide quality continuing education at an affordable price." They deliver 500,000 courses annually, and offer state-specific courses focusing on annuities, long-term care, law and ethics for all 50 states and Washington, D.C. They offer online and paper-based course delivery options. To enroll, visit the URL provided previously, or call them at 1-800-488-9308 to speak with one of their representatives.

You need to sign up and start studying immediately. Most of these classes only take about one week to complete, and we've actually had motivated new agents pass the test in two days. We have also had people that take six months to get it done. It's your choice as to how fast you want to get started. If you ask me, I say start fast. Fast creates momentum, and "the big Mo" covers errors. If you are anxious to make money, to build a large team of professionals, to become an agency manager, then you should be anxious to get licensed and start with the NAA team. Each state has licensing requirements and you can receive a reciprocal license in each state where you intend to work. This is a pretty simple process that just requires some paperwork and a license fee. In some states the license is very inexpensive at around $25, while other states might be as much as $250. We highly recommend that you first get your license in the state where you live, and then follow up by getting licensed in the states that connect to your state. This reminds me of a guy who told me that he only wanted to buy land connected to his land in the United States. The funny thing about this is, if he followed that pattern and kept buying, he would eventually own the entire country. If you follow his lead, then you will end up being licensed in all 50 states. That's the goal, and this puts you on the path of being able to sell life insurance and annuities all over the country.

Now that you have your license, the key is to get rolling out of the gate. It's like a sprint. You do not want to hesitate out of the gate or the race is already lost.

Even if you don't have your license, you can still get started. It is called building your outlets. In other words, start making a list.

RECIPE FOR SUCCESS

INGREDIENTS:

THE LIST:

- The most important thing about a list is you need to start making it NOW!

- If you are fortunate enough to have a manager that is willing to call your list of names for you, that is incredible; or if you have a big agency manager that is growing like crazy and wishes to call your people for you, that's even better. My suggestion is to HURRY UP! The Managers want to help you. Get them calling while they are interested in your list. If you are in the situation that many people are, and you have to call your own list, that is OK too. No person ever called my list for me and many of our managers have become very successful calling their own list in the beginning. So, either way, get started.

> *"I've discovered that who stirs the pot has an impact on what's in the pot."*
>
> –Jon Gordon,
> **best-selling author
> of SOUP**

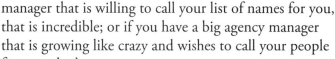

IDEAS FOR PUTTING A LIST TOGETHER:

Success results when preparedness (your contacts) meets opportunity (selling great products). It is a numbers game.

The more people you can put on your list, the greater your chances of success. You now have great financial products to share with your friends, family, and contacts!

Most often, the more successful a person is already, then the faster they are going to see the tremendous opportunity that you can now offer. Remember, you are doing them a favor—they are not doing you a favor. You are offering the opportunity for financial security —the opportunity to help a person help themself while helping others.

Be sure not to prejudge the people on your list—especially successful people. When you think, "Oh, they wouldn't be interested," you just made a decision for that person—a decision that deprives them of the greatest opportunity to get the best financial products in the country. Give them their freedom to decide. Then, they can never say you didn't give them a chance. Many people will thank you for the rest of their lives. Prejudging can cost you insane amounts of money!

Consider The Following:

- Friends
- Neighbors
- Relatives
- Church Members
- Fellow Employees
- Club Members
- Past Associates
- Christmas Card List
- Wedding Invitation List (If married)
- Classmates
- Anyone you admire (Even if you don't know them well, they want money and security, too)

NOTE: Begin jotting names down immediately!!! Put the names

down on paper as soon as you think of them. The more credible a person is the faster their potential to understand the quality of what we offer. Show your products to the sharpest, most successful people you know or meet.

Who Do You Know?

As long as you know people, you know people with needs. Needs lead to sales!!! To get started, to give direction, ASK WHO DO I KNOW THAT...

- I respect
- Shows genuine concern for other people
- Is active in their church
- People always seem to like
- Does personal counseling, such as leaders, doctors, lawyers, etc.
- Is a professional
- Is in clubs and various group organizations or active in civic affairs
- Is in a teaching position in a school or business
- Deals with the public: policeman, fireman, postman, city official
- Is in a manager, supervisor, consultant or trainer capacity
- Is looking for more out of life
- Is ambitious, aggressive and "on the go"
- Is considered a leader
- Has children just starting junior high, high school or college
- Has children with special talents that should be developed

- Wants to set a good example for their children to follow
- Owns their own business
- Holds very responsible positions that are causing stress and pressure on them
- Wants to have freedom
- Is considering a new profession or changing jobs, or recently changed jobs
- Is unable to advance on their job
- Has talents but is held back
- Just started selling or is an experienced direct salesman
- Relies on ideas for his livelihood—authors, designers, promoters, advertisers, etc.
- Has never been able to get started or failed in business but still has strong desires
- Is going to college, business school, trade school, etc. or just graduated
- Was recently married and is just "starting out"

"Do you own all the products you are offering others?"

POM POM: PLENTY OF MONEY AND PEACE OF MIND

Help others get what they need, Protect their family, Realize their dreams! It is a natural human trait when you have sincerely sold yourself on the great products you have to offer.

It is psychologically impossible to keep a "good thing" to yourself. Everyone has the compulsion to "spread the good word." When you want to grow even bigger and stronger, start being friendly to everyone you meet and that will add a few hundred more names to your list. They will thank you!

Who:

- Works with the rescue squad
- Control company
- Owns beach/mountain cottage where we vacationed
- Sells us gas and services our car
- Sold my wife her wig
- Works downtown
- Owns a nursery
- Delivers parcel post packages (UPS)
- Works with an exterminating pest control
- Stores my wife's winter coat
- Sells ice cream in the neighborhood
- Owns or manages the jewelry store
- Sells aluminum awnings
- Works for a travel agency

WE KNOW SOMEONE WHO IS A...

Nurse	Police detective	PBX operator	Librarian
Music teacher	Golf pro	Grocery store owner	Social worker
Mortician	Farmer	Student	Insurance adjustor
Art instructor	Race car driver	Missionary	Fashion model
Warehouse manager	Moving van operator	Fisherman	Security guard
Pediatrician	Auto stereo dealer	Coin dealer	Sheriff
Prof. ball player	Furniture dealer	Tool & Die maker	Fire chief
Cookware salesman	Dance instructor	Sawmill operator	Secretary
Industrial engineer	Researcher	Telephone lineman	Lithographer
Welder	Bench machinist	Waiter/Waitress	Actor
Land clearer	Crane operator	Horse trader	Statistician

Cement finisher	Candy salesman	Antique dealer	Brewery salesman
Contractor	Forester	Chiropractor	Podiatrist
Seamstress	Optometrist	Architect	Dental hygienist
Carpenter	Shoe repairman	Physical therapist	Motel/Hotel owner
Pilot/Stewardess	Highway patrolman	Judge	Photographer/Model
Bus driver	Pizza delivery	Car wash owner	Door salesman
Bank cashier/teller	Water delivery	Caterer	Veterinarian
Video store owner	Cloth cutter	Boat salesman	Sells fire wood
Gutter cleaner	Garage mechanic	Hot tub salesman	insulation installer
Editor	Lab technician	Restaurant owner	Paper Mill worker
Brick mason	Drafting manager	Printer	Office manager
Bakery owner	Plant foreman	Dietician	Mechanic
Anesthetist	Surgeon	Real estate agency	Railroad ticket agent
Newspaper pressman	Bulldozer operator	Mobile home sales	Soft drink distributor
Air traffic controller	Lifeguard	Swimming teacher	Interior decorator

List Building by Free Association

- You should get your spouse to make a list also. And your children…they know people!

- When you read (hear) each word, write the first name that comes into your mind.

- Please do not stop to prejudge the person or consider if they would be interested.

A Simple List might look like this:

	Name	Number	State
•	Name	Number	State
•	John Doe	555-1234	N.C.
•	Suzy Smith	578-9834	Fla.
•	Bobby Riggins	935-8034	Texas
•	Laura Williams	877-3511	Ohio

You can come up with even more names using the description list. It's basically 100-plus descriptions like bald, chef, smart, tall, etc…that you can use to help come up with more names.

As you can see this list builder sheet is very simple. In today's world there is Facebook, Google+, Twitter, and databases on your cell phone filled with people that you know.

You can locate anybody on Facebook, and there are so many ways to generate a list that you really have no excuse not to have a large list. You can start with one name and telephone number, or you can wait until you have 20 names and numbers or 200.

The number of people really doesn't matter, but the sooner that you get started, the faster you are going to make something happen.

The secret here? START!

Social Media can help you produce a list of contacts—maybe you haven't seen the people in 20 years, but you still know these people and you can get in touch with them using all these different avenues. Start calling and contacting people.

The key is to start calling people and find out the answer to one of these two questions: Are they interested in a tax-free retirement and life insurance policy where they can protect their family, and are they interested in making an income outside of the business they are currently in? A list is the raw materials to the rest of your life. It is the substance that gets you started.

If you understand the value of one person that buys a policy is possibly $200, $1,000, or possibly $20,000 from one sale, then that should be incentive enough to build a large list. In addition to that, this person could possibly become one of your top sales guys or one of your top agency builders. This could create hundreds of thousands of dollars in income over your life and therefore, one of the biggest investments you've ever made. All FREE by you just putting together a list! Generate a large list and use that list to make money to create a bigger list and a bigger team.

POWER OF THE PIPELINE

When I refer to building a system, I am reminded of a story about two brothers who were looking for a job on a small island that had some water flow issues. As the two brothers looked for a job, they finally found one carrying buckets of water from one of the few fresh wells to a huge feeding trough at a restaurant on the island. The one man looked at his brother and told him how lucky they were to have found work, and he thought it was amazing. He was so happy. He said, "Thank God we have a job!"

The other brother wasn't so pleased. He looked at the blisters on his hands, felt the sunburn on his back and shoulders, and he said, "Are you kidding me?"

The first brother said, "We are better off than a lot of people are." I agree with that brother. The positive brother had a bigger dream and was already thinking about building a pipeline that would take a long time to build, but one that would eventually supply water all over the island. What about that?

Yes, it's going to take a long, long time to build, but that brother knew if they started working on it now (in other words, "MOVE"), then they could get it done over time and eventually live a better life.

We've all heard the saying, "inch by inch, anything's a cinch." We could take that approach and, inch by inch, put a pipeline in. Once this pipeline is completed, we would end up like the brothers who had an endless water supply on the island, only our pipeline would flow with money and not water. It reminds me of a person who is willing to put in extra effort and build a cash flow system of money coming in. Those brothers could have gotten more buckets or even bigger buckets, but that just leads to heavier loads and it's still a temporary fix.

The pipeline is the best solution. Once you build one pipeline, a smart person would probably build a second pipeline too. From there, you continue to add more lines! It resembles playing games. Some people play checkers and there are some people that play chess. There are also people that play Hacky Sack. It's just a matter of the level you are thinking on.

What level are you on?

Are you a planner?

Even if you are neither a thinker nor a planner, can you copy a system and strategy that has worked in the past? Can you take instructions on how to think long-term to build a pipeline that brings the water ($$$money$$$) in on a regular basis?

Often people say they don't have the personality to build or run an organization. Much like the pipeline that we've built, it isn't about the personality, it's about the execution. It's digging the hole to lay the pipe and having the right angle on the pipe that is important. Heck, you can learn to lay the pipe by following a simple blueprint.

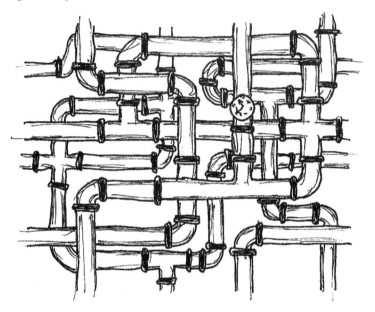

That takes the personality out of the equation, and shows that a person with little charisma or personality can still build an organization. As a matter of fact, when you look at professional athletes, movie stars, or a particular business that is based on the personality or charisma, often times their careers and time in the spotlight is short lived. You probably think of Colonel Harland Sanders when you hear the name KFC (Kentucky Fried Chicken). The Colonel had the character, but you realize it was his sauce—11 secret herbs and spices—and his chicken-cooking method that made his business successful.

It wasn't his signature white suit, black tie, or white facial hair that he wore religiously until his death at age 90 that made him millions. It was the chicken and his ability to teach others how to mass produce it! The fact that it could be duplicated by others in thousands and thousands of stores worldwide is why you remember his personality. His image is what got him recognized, but it did not build system, machine, and the pipeline. Hard work and persistent effort is what got him the pipeline. Yes, it is tougher to dig the trench from the well to the restaurant than to carry the bucket, but it's a one-time work and not a forever work. Even if you have to pay a plumber or fix leaks from time to time, it is miniscule maintenance compared to continually filling up buckets of water. A friend of mine once used the following analogy: If you are out in the jungle cutting weeds down, then it's going to take forever to chop your way out of that jungle by yourself. Now, if we had a team of people, say our corporate staff or our leaders—all with machetes—then we could chop our way out much faster. What we are attempting to do is to cut away not just a path or country road, but more of a super highway of success. I mean a nice wide highway with concrete or blacktop, with clear yellow lines to follow, and blinking signs that lead the way.

What exactly are we trying to create? We want a business that doesn't create negativity. We want a business with no confusion because when a person is confused they tend not to act. Chaos often creates misguided behavior toward other people. We do not want people acting with misdirected emotions. We desire uniformity and teamwork. People will get discouraged and quit if they see internal confusion. Our system is designed to help people hang on one more day for that this-might-be-the-day moment when the pipeline pushes through the last, hard rock blocking the path. We want to create a business where the money continually flows. You want to build a business where the pipeline (a proven system) is clear of all debris (confusion, chaos, and colossal catastrophes).

> *"Opportunities are usually disguised as hard work, so most people don't recognize them."*
>
> –Ann Landers

Rest assured, when you see a turtle on a fence post, the one thing you know for sure is that he did not get there by himself.

That joker had some help from somebody or multiple people to get him off the ground and onto that post top. Our system was not built by a turtle, but it was built by many helping hands over time. Our leaders have spent hundreds of hours formulating the plan. It was manpower, consulting, and teamwork that built our system. We know it's not perfect. We will tell you that right now, but it's always evolving and changing. We take suggestions from our newcomers, as well as our veteran growers and builders. We are disciplined engineers, and we will test a program to see if it works. If it works, we will put it in our system. You can send us suggestions to www.suggestions@naaleads.com. Every suggestion—100%—will be read, and we implement ideas that we find effective. We believe in creating a system that works and is an ever-growing, finely-tuned machine.

As I looked at our company, I always asked people to keep it simple and do things based on the way I had seen success. When I studied other insurance companies, marketing companies, small general agencies and captive companies—big and small, I concluded that they didn't seem to have a system. I don't know of another organization that has a clear-cut description of how to run every aspect of their business like National Agents Alliance does. I wanted to create a system in the life insurance and annuity business that was unlike any other. I wanted NAA to be a company that allowed a salesperson, an aspiring salesperson, or an aspiring franchisee to join us. I wanted a proven time-tested system that would help these people survive and even thrive.

There is no doubt that the next 20 years in this industry will offer the largest wealth transfer in the history of our country. Statistics show that the first Baby Boomer turned 65 on Jan. 1, 2011. For the next 19 years, 10,000 people are turning 65 every single day as the Baby Boomer Generation ages. That's a lot of people, and they have a lot of money they need to do something with. We know this statistic is true: 100% of all people leave their wealth behind because they can't take it with them. The Baby Boomer Generation is a huge market and a great opportunity for us to present retirement solutions to people who just do NOT know the best ways to protect their money. Our challenge is to teach them the proper way to transfer their assets to future generations, and to do so with the fewest tax consequences. *Millionaire Maker Manual* is designed to train agents who can safely provide clear direction, ample motivation, and precise directions for producing for our clients a pipeline of positive cash flow. The better our agents serve our clients, the bigger their own pipelines can become.

"Opportunity is missed by most people because it is dressed in overalls and looks like work."

–Thomas A. Edison

We have seen this kind of success in our organization from school teachers, mortgage brokers, bankers, secretaries, fast-food chain workers, horse trainers, engineers, athletes, and just about any other type of professional you can name. We have a system that anybody can tap into and have enough success where they can duplicate themselves to build a huge business; a business where they eventually have a duplication factor of 100%. Then, they will have created a factory of financial success and their own cash flow pipeline.

Power of the Pipeline

- DUPLICATES—does not innovate
- Predictable as the day is long
- Momentum overcomes errors
- Scorecards and scoreboards are easy to watch
- A destination is clearly defined
- Organizations have exponential growth
- You make money while you make money … while you make money
- Expands nationally
- Creates urgency
- Builds capacity
- Takes the lid off limits
- Increases depth of understanding
- Leverages time
- Compounds the cash flow
- Smooths out inefficiencies
- Changes people's lives for the better

"You can have everything in life that you want if you will just help enough people get what they want."

–Zig Ziglar

AGENCY MANAGER

OUR BEGINNING, YOUR BEGINNING

At the AGENCY MANAGER and OASys-approved levels (NAA's Online Lead Allocation System) you run your own base shop. You now have the foundation to build a huge business and YOU must be the catalyst that propels each of your agents to follow the system, so they can also reach the level of Agency Manager. This position comes with greater responsibility. You must now spend more time training and guiding an ever-growing team of professionals who will rely on you for their progress as an independent business owner. You can build your NAA hierarchy as big as you want it, and your leadership is crucial to its success. Without doubt, you can expect to work harder than ever, but the financial reward will be worth the effort.

You'll be the one ordering leads for your business AND for your growing team. You have a charge to run team meetings, promote HotSpots, and set the example by attending EVERY corporate event. This is the moment where you make the decision to be the next big star in our organization by continuing strong personal production, providing field training for new agents, and ramping up recruiting activity within your team. Do this and you will create a massive base and you will develop future Agency Managers in width and depth.

Each AGENCY MANAGER you have in width and depth creates the potential for you to earn bonuses provided by the company. The more qualified Agency Managers your hierarchy has, the more income recognition, and trust you have earned within the organization. If you have a burning desire to succeed and truly follow the system, you can hit this level in six months or less. The record right now is 90 days, and we hope that you are the person that beats this mark!

AGENCY MANAGER STRUCTURE

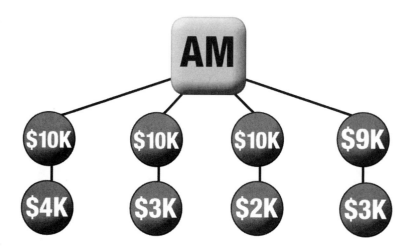

COOKIE CUTTER AGENCY MANAGERS

Think of your ability to break out agency managers as a "cookie-cutter" model. There is a simple description given for all the levels you need to progress through to reach the AGENCY MANAGER level and to duplicate, like a "cookie-cutter," more and more AGENCY MANAGERS. Whether you are an INDEPENDENT BUSINESS ASSOCIATE (IBA) or a DOUBLE DIAMOND LEADER (DDL), it's all mapped out for you. Follow the system and do the work to reach each progressive level demonstrated. Step-by-step you'll work your way up to AGENCY MANAGER (and beyond) and soon you can be creating new AGENCY MANAGERS just like you.

Currently, we have the following levels at NAA:

(See the following pages)

AGENT LEVELS CHART

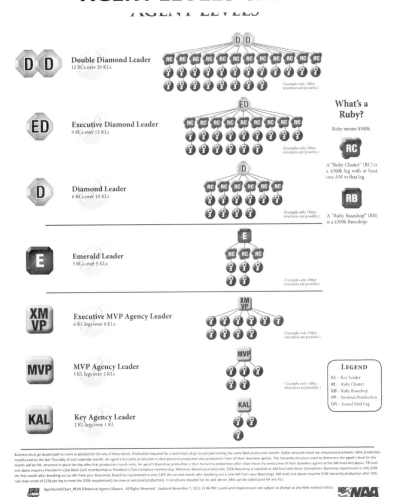

The first three levels are about as easy to reach as they could possibly be. When you get started as an agent, you get your license, and when your first application has been issued paid, you become an INDEPENDENT BUSINESS ASSOCIATE (IBA). That's your first step, and as the ancient Chinese Proverb states: "A journey of a thousand miles starts with one step!" Now, just latch on to

AGENT LEVELS CHART

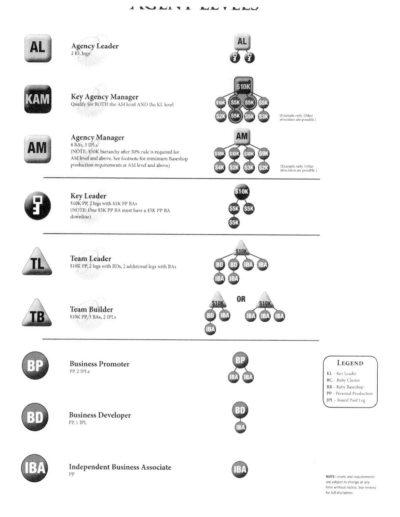

AGENT LEVELS

that mindset. If you can sell one policy, you are on your way to becoming a millionaire! Keep doing what you just did.

Now that you have personal production, when you help a new agent get a policy issued paid, you become a BUSINESS DEVELOPER (BD), and you have started building your team. Help a second agent get started and get issued paid production and you are promoted to BUSINESS PROMOTER (BP) (see AGENT LEVELS chart).

Your next goal is to attain TEAM BUILDER (TB) status. The requirements are $10,000 per month in personal production, and a team structure with two BDs with at least one IBA in depth, or the team structure could be three IBAs in width under you, along with the $10,000 in personal production (see AGENT LEVELS chart). Membership in NAA's President's Club Black Card or Complete is required at this level and beyond. The BIG key here is that you personally produce a minimum of $10,000 issued paid business each month.

TEAM LEADER

TEAM LEADER (TL) is the next level to achieve. In addition to your $10,000 in personal production, your team will have a minimum of two BDs and two additional IBAs in width. Keep selling, keep recruiting. You are moving up through the Agent Levels!

KEY LEADER

You are now very close to reaching a really important level with NAA, which was rolled out in 2011, and has been vital in growing the company. The KEY LEADER (KL) position can be accomplished in a reasonable amount of time and requires $10,000 per month in personal production and two legs with a minimum of three agents each producing $5,000 per month with one of the two legs having one agent in depth.

KEY LEADER STRUCTURE

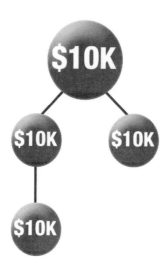

AGENCY MANAGERS

Now you are ready to make that big step to AGENCY MANAGER (AM), and this position requires eight IBAs, at least three Issued Paid Legs (IPLs), $50,000 total hierarchy issued paid premium after the 50 percent rule (only $25,000 in production from any one leg counts toward the $50,000), and, if you have other AGENCY MANAGERS in your downline, have at least $25,000 issued paid premium in your baseshop (your team). An example of the structure that would qualify as AGENCY MANAGER would have five agents in at least two Issued Paid Legs, each agent having at least $5,000 in personal production for the month, plus a leg with a KEY LEADER in it in the same month. That's one example; there are other possible structures to reach this level. (see AGENT LEVELS chart)

MOVING UP

Now that you have earned the AGENCY MANAGER level your goal is to start your "cookie-cutter" assembly line producing AGENCY MANAGERS in your downline. As you continue building a bigger and bigger business you will advance one step at a time through the remaining eight levels until you become a DOUBLE DIAMOND LEADER.

As you're building your hierarchy, study the graphics we've included in this section to see what it takes to reach each successive level. The system is in place for you to advance beyond where you are today, with no limits on your income. You decide where you want to go. Take the "cookie-cutter" and pop out AGENCY MANAGER after AGENCY MANAGER. Identify the person with potential, work with that agent, help them build, and teach them to lead their team. You teach them to build it, you help them build it, and you guide them along the way. Now identify another winner and teach them. Keep developing AGENCY MANAGERS and you will climb to the top and create the life you dream about. Focus on the model that's been laid out for you. Create and cultivate your hierarchy by following the system. Study the graphics included here. The system that has proven successful is your friend. If you are serious about building this business and you stick to the system, you can qualify as an AGENCY MANAGER very quickly. The typical time for someone with a burning desire to succeed is about six months. Think about creating AGENCY MANAGERS in width just like you would purchase additional McDonald's franchises; more outlets equal more revenue. More AGENCY MANAGERS equals more revenue in your business.

THE QUESTION IS THIS:

- How many can you build in width and how many can you build in depth?

- What is your desire?

- What is the level of your dream?

- How big do you want your business to be?
- How important do you want to be with National Agents Alliance?
- How much recognition do you want?
- What is the size of the distribution system that you would like to have?
- How much do you want to give away... to your church or different charities?
- How many families in need do you want to help?
- What standard do you want to set for others to follow?
- Just how big is your vision?

NAA has given you the path to run on. Follow the path. Now RUN!

HOW TO GO FROM 1 TO 11 IN ONE STEP

When you recruit a new agent, the process of building a strong working relationship with that person begins, and it is the perfect time to meet the spouse. Bringing the spouse into the discussion in the very beginning will reap huge future dividends for you and your new agent.

We have statistically proven that with agent and spouse sitting side by side, both excited about their new business, there is an 11 times greater possibility of success than with just the agent alone. Having the spouse "on-board" and 100 percent committed to the business is extremely important, because, typically, a husband and wife have a huge impact on the attitude and behavior of each other. When obstacles pop up in the business, and they always do, there will be a strong support system of encouragement between the spouses that will not allow defeat. Will there be tough times when the agent and/or the spouse want to quit? Sure, but when one person is down, the other can provide the firewall to prevent the problem from spreading. As long as they both don't quit on the same day, they'll work through any problems, and their business will thrive.

Through building the business relationship with this new couple, we sometimes discover that the spouse of the recruit is actually BEST suited for building the NAA business model and takes the lead role. They also double your potential network because each of them has their own "circle of influence," and the warm market they bring to the table may be totally different.

You can now see the benefits of this powerful partnership and how having the support of the spouse can be such a positive force on the business, and will help minimize any potential problems. ALWAYS find ways to implement this NAA philosophy when you bring on a new agent. Your odds of success can be increased from 1 to 11 with this one simple step.

RAW MATERIALS

"Stop playing billy goat business! Stop letting your butt get in the way. When people tell me, 'But this…But that…But I…' I have to smile at them. They say, 'you don't understand the circumstances I am under or the situation I am in.' Your 'butt' may be getting in the way! Please stop 'butting' me Billy! The choices you make are far more important than the circumstances you are in! Please choose to listen and do, instead of 'baaing' and butting."

–Andy Albright

INVEST IN YOU

YOU ARE YOUR FIRST RECRUIT!

Early in the process, one of the things—a major thing—that a person needs to do is get educated about their business and become aware of all the resources that are available to ensure their success. I would advise them to head to www.ShopAtNAA.com and see the literature that is available for purchase. A lot of items are available for free but you have to get them from the carriers. Some of the items, like CDs, books, brochures, or anything of credibility related to your company you will need to purchase. Wanting to build a business for free is a normal, novel idea, but realistically you need to invest in your business and build your personal inventory of books, CDs, and training materials. You need to have your business structured so that when you grow, you can hand these materials to other people.

IF YOU HAD TO INVEST IN ONE PERSON ON EARTH WHO WOULD YOU INVEST IN?

A lot of mothers, when they are asked this question, say "their children." Well, if you are on Southwest airlines, they tell you in the event that the cabin losses pressure, you should put the oxygen mask on yourself first! Then, you can worry about a child. If you have two children, then you have to decide which of your children to put the mask on first. They tell you to put the mask on yourself first because if you are dead, then you cannot help anybody else.

You need this mentality in business and in life. That child depends on you, and can't survive if you are not around. Why is this so hard for adults to comprehend? You should, without hesitation, start thinking that you are the first person on Earth you would bet on, invest in, and trust. If you don't think that way, how are you going to convince others to follow and believe in you?

> *"The quality of a person's life is in direct proportion to their commitment to excellence, regardless of their chosen field of endeavor."*
>
> **–Green Bay Packers Coach Vince Lombardi**

If you cannot convince yourself that you are great, then you are in trouble. If you start betting on yourself, then you will be amazed at how differently people begin to look at you, and they will respect you more. Do yourself a favor and start living that way. I am amazed at people that don't invest in their own interests and then wait for something to be on sale. If something is $100, then they are waiting on you to offer it to them for $50. If you know that it's worth $100, then why are you waiting to get it?

If your life depended on it, would you wait??? You would not flinch!

Who would you trust most in this world? If the answer is not YOU, then there is a problem. The answer should be you! There should be no person in the world that you count on more than yourself.

I was in a coliseum with thousands of people listening to Bill Britt talk about how the majority of millionaires in the world have read two books: the *Bible* and *Think and Grow Rich*. Britt was pushing those books, but he was talking about always "investing in you." I went to another seminar with Brian Tracy and he said the same thing. About five seminars later, I kept hearing it over and over again…Invest in YOU!!! It's a simple thought, but people have trouble grasping the concept. I paid thousands and thousands of dollars to hear that message over and over.

I can remember reading anything—and everything—could get my hands on from insurance carriers. I watched videos, listened to MP3s and CDs. Whatever I could find, I soaked it all in. Some of it was free, but I was willing to pay for that information because it was only going to help me with my business, so it made sense to me to get it and use it. That's the mentality you should have. You should be willing to invest in you because you know it is the right thing to do.

The more often you invest in you, the more willing others will be to invest in you and themselves, as their business grows. The sooner you believe this, the better off you will be.

I will bet I invest more than anybody in the tools and system we have at our disposal. I give people business tools all the time, because I love it when people show me they are committed. If a person is willing to put some "skin in the game," I am more likely to invest my time, efforts, and emotion into them.

HOW TO DRAW OUT YOUR TEAM

When you begin to draw out your team, you start with a blank sheet of white paper. You want to draw out your team from the top left of the paper to the right side. Think about your strongest people and decide who your top person is. You are going to start on the left side because that is how you read. Your natural instinct is to go immediately to the top left first.

Write out your team of people across the top of the page. You are going to have to figure out who is stronger business-wise rather than who you may like more. People on the far left are those who appear to be listening, "moving," and ideally working the system. You must realize that you are trying to lock in on the "best" people.

Are they great at recruiting? Do they sell more than they recruit? Can they do both?

You have to figure out what you are looking for and rank people based on that. Don't think about it too long. You should be able to just throw out a name and know where they would rank.

If you know that dealing with certain people is going to be more difficult than with others, you probably want them at the far right of your list, or you may eventually get to a point where they are not on your list anymore. There are just some people you cannot help because they will find every excuse in the world not to do something. Those are not the people you want to work with. You want people who are ready to "move."

You want to find people that are "READY, WILLING, AND ABLE."

Drawing out your team is like a baseball manager making out a lineup card. The great thing is that players on your bench are only one play from being in your starting lineup, and your starters are one play from being on the bench. It constantly changes from day to day.

Why is drawing out your team important? It's a defined way to visually show you which people you need to invest your time with, and it shows you those you need to spend less time with. You want to work more with people that are more profitable, easier to coach, more receptive, and more productive. You want to work less with the people that are difficult to coach, not responsive to the system, and lack productivity.

Two things that will affect your team layout and where you place people on it are:

- A person who does really well will move up and to the left

- A person who doesn't really work will move down and to the right

AFFECTS ON YOUR TEAM DIAGRAM

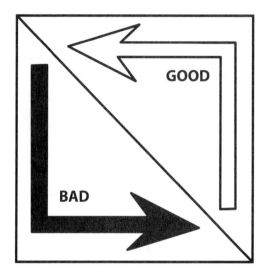

Will the act of drawing out your team lead to competition? Yes! People, by nature, want to be at the far left of your layout. Share this diagram with your team. Show them how you draw it out. Tell them why you draw it out. Your decisions on this should be deliberate, effective, simple, and straightforward.

A lot of people do not even think to rank things in their life. You should draw things out, not only with your team, but with other areas of your life. NAA has three main areas that we use as indicators. We like to work with people that want to have fun, make money, and make a difference.

We like to find people that actually do these three things in life. We really do believe in the principles taught by Napoleon Hill in *Think and Grow Rich* regarding the importance of having a positive attitude. Hill wrote, "There is no hope for success for the person who repels people through a negative personality." Stay away from negative people…they will drag your business down! Another quote from Hill's classic book states, "The man…whose personality is such that he gets along with all kinds of people…has a most decided edge…" Find the WINNERS in your hierarchy and spend your time and efforts with them. The NAA way is to operate from a servant's heart, and service will be returned to you exponentially. When you are cooperative, others will cooperate. Leading this way will set the example for your hierarchy and will eliminate envy, jealousy, and selfishness, and therefore your team will follow you.

So, let's just say you draw out a team of five people across the top of the page. You know their order, so now you have to go under them and identify the strongest people under them in depth. One way to do that is to put a star or a circle around their name that makes them stand out from the others on that level. Who is the star on that second level? From there, you can continue working down at each level.

DRAWING YOUR TEAM OUT DIAGRAM

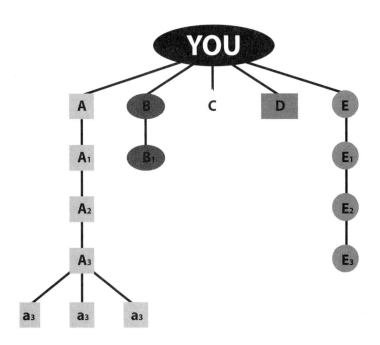

WHY IS IT IMPORTANT TO DRAW OUT YOUR TEAM?

- Helps keep your goals in mind
- Reminds you of what you are ranking (production, recruiting, etc.)
- Helps you make solid, clear decisions on who to work with
- Shows people chasing your top producers what they're shooting for
- Shows exactly where you need to place some bold, new agents
- Helps you clearly see the strengths and weaknesses of your organization
- Helps you determine who needs additional training and in what areas

Doing this activity every day will help you be successful and create other successes. The successful person knows what they have done, but others, especially newer agents, might not realize when they have done a great job. It is important to recognize others that are doing a great job. By drawing out your hierarchy every day you will know who should receive recognition.

Most winners work harder than others. Some new agents might ask: "How do I work harder?" That's a great question! When winners hear a person say, "I want to work smarter, not harder," they scratch their head and think, "that's a loser's mentality." Most winners want to figure out how to work harder and accomplish more. When I say harder, I do not mean physical exhaustion, a person that is out of breath, doing back-breaking work. I'm talking about harder in terms of figuring out how to find more hours.

For example, if I had a jet that allowed me to work more hours without wasting as many hours in airports, and allowed me to get to and from places faster, then I'd get more accomplished. Some people find it harder to think in those terms, but that is how most big winners think. They want to do more work, but they're going to work more effectively and more efficiently. We want people who want to work!

Winners are **BOLDER** than most people, and that is what separates them from being average. Bold thinking and the ability to think outside the box allows people to get ahead, to work harder in a more focused manner, and to lead by example.

When former PGA Tour champion Lee Trevino was growing up in Texas as a not-so-well-off teenager, he quit school at age 14 to make $30 a day carrying other people's clubs and shining shoes. He would sneak on the courses to practice and play the game he loved when he was not caddying.

At age 17, Trevino enlisted in the United States Marine Corps. He spent a good deal of time during the next four years playing golf with other officers, and they encouraged him to play professional golf. He went on to win six major titles—including wins in the U.S. Open, British Open, and PGA Championship.

Trevino says that he never would have made it in golf had he not done one particular thing every single day when he was playing as a young man, hustling just to scratch out a living. "You've got to be willing to bet everything you have in your pocket every day," Trevino told the Golf Channel in 2011. "If you don't think you'll win, your attitude is wrong." In fact, Trevino tells of days he bet money he didn't even have in his pocket and he HAD to win. That's real pressure!

The man they call "The Merry Mex" or "Supermex" knew early on that he was going to COMMIT and put everything he had into what he was doing.

On a trip with Mutual of Omaha, I spent some time with Jeff Heller, Mutual of Omaha's Chairman of the Board. He talked about his many years of building different businesses, and he talked to me about people that worked outside of the box, people that were willing to build a team, and people willing to do things that are out of the ordinary. Heller told me that one of his favorite people to work with was H. Ross Perot, a Texas businessman and 1992 presidential candidate. According to Heller, Perot was big on hiring people right out of the Vietnam War, people with leadership skills, people that were independent, people that were not afraid to work 24/7, and people that would keep fighting even against all odds. This has to be one of the bolder, more aggressive moves that I've ever heard of a company making. Today, Perot Systems is still one of Perot's success stories as he continues to make billions after selling off Electronic Data Systems (EDS) in 1984 for $2.5 billion. Yes, working harder and being bolder paid off for those guys. We love that mindset and we feel like National Agents Alliance can follow a similar strategy to help take us to being a billion-dollar company.

> *"Showing up is important and it is a big part of becoming successful."*
>
> –Andy Albright

COMPOUNDING YOUR INVESTMENT

To grow your business you must become financially literate. If you don't understand money, how can you run your business? We want our agents to learn how to run profitable businesses and not end up in the red. We've seen too many companies fail in the last few years all over the United States, just because the business owner didn't understand the basics of money management.

When you read your financials, do you understand them? You have to learn how to see trends, see where you need to spend more and see where you shouldn't spend at all. It's the little things that can make all the difference in you being successful. You want to make money! You are not doing this to lose money!

YOU CAN'T SAVE YOUR WAY TO WEALTH

You just can't do it. You have to invest your wealth. Clipping coupons, getting a low-interest return on your savings account, and looking for deals will not lead to financial freedom.

Getting a return on your investment is a huge concept to understand. When I put money into something, I expect to get some type of return on that investment. It's hard to get people to understand this, but having cash in a bank is not an asset for you. It is an asset for the bank. The bank is using that money, not you! You're getting a set percent of return on leaving money there and you'll be taxed on it annually, while banks are leveraging that money for their own gains. More and more banks don't keep money in-house; they're making it work for them at your expense.

If you keep leaving your money in places where it yields only a marginal return, you are not making money off of it. You're actually losing money after taxes in a lot of cases. Why make one percent, when you can find a 10 percent return elsewhere.

Percentages either work for you or against you!!! They'll be positive or negative. These are some of the money basics you have to know.

> *"In order to get wealthy in this world you can't do so as an employee or being self-employed. The wealthy of this world became wealthy through being a business owner or being an investor."*
>
> –Robert Kiyosaki, **author of** *Rich Dad, Poor Dad*

How often does your money double in a typical interest-bearing account?

An important concept to understand regarding compounding your money is known as the "Rule of 72." This rule will help you calculate how quickly you can double your money. Divide 72 by the interest rate you are earning and the result is the number of years it will take to double your money at that rate. For example is you are earning 10 percent interest, divide 72 by 10 and you would double your money in 7.2 years. Or, you could divide by the number of years in which you would like to double your money and the answer is the interest rate you would have to have to accomplish your goal. Say you wanted to double your money in eight years, divide 72 by eight and you can see it would take nine-percent interest to double your money.

When you have to consider taxes in the equation you might have to use a factor of, say, 108 instead of 72. If you have one-percent interest coming to you, then it will only take you 108 years to double your money! Wealthy people aren't on that program! They don't get wealthy by just putting money in a savings account at a one-percent interest level.

Let's say you want to build a big agency. What if you invest $100 in a newspaper advertisement to find new agents and it yields a 108 percent return for you? In only a year, you would double your money if you stayed on that track.

If you are a personal producer and don't have any desire to build a team, then you take your commissions and invest them somewhere. That's how you are going to get wealthy. If you work a normal 9-to-5 job, you either develop your own side business or you become an investor. Most of those people start as business owners and move to investor because they learn how money grows.

The wealthy of the world are the people smart enough to change their thoughts on money and find ways to compound their money.

SO-CALLED MONEY GURUS ARE GENIUSES FOR THE MASSES

Dave Ramsey is great, and his books are good reads. He talks about paying off debt and staying debt-free. That's a great concept, and I'm all for that. His radio shows are great, and he has good advice for the "Joe Common" out there. However, Dave Ramsey is like most "money gurus." Those guys are geniuses for the masses. If you get "back to broke" that's great. However, it would be ideal if you worked your budget to where you were able to reinvest in your business and have your assets grow!

"I have a problem with too much money. I can't reinvest it fast enough, and because I reinvest it, more money comes in. Yes, the rich do get richer."

–Robert Kiyosaki

Ben Franklin was right when he said, "A penny saved is a penny earned." Franklin, however, didn't have to live in the world we do. What if you don't totally pay off a credit card, but instead invest in your business and get a higher ROI (Return On Investment). Over time, you could actually make more money than if you used that money to completely pay off debts and had no money to invest in your business. People like Ramsey are talking to the masses that are probably never going to earn any significant income. It might be $30,000 to $50,000 annually. That's Ramsey's target audience and he's great at it; that's why he's rich. Our target market is middle-class America. That's who we serve. By serving middle America, we get paid extremely well. I don't know what Dave Ramsey's income is like, but I doubt that he did all that he does—books, radio show, etc...—without going into debt at some point. I'd almost bet you that he had to go into debt to get his empire rolling! Do you think he did that debt free? I don't! Ramsey built a business and I will bet you that he invested in it too!

Guys, I'm not saying be reckless with your money. I think you should be smart about it, but I also think you have to invest in your business for the long haul. If you do that you can get a payoff down the road that will be more valuable than getting out of debt right now. Use the capital you have right now to grow your business and watch the payoff you get.

Investing could mean that you are buying ads. It could mean you are hiring administrative staff to handle paperwork. Either way it's an investment and it's the way I built my business. There is no telling how much of a return you will get from investing, let's say $1,000 in your business. If you pay off a $1,000 credit card debt you know exactly what you are getting. You paid off $1,000 and you don't owe that anymore. You also don't have that $1,000 you could use in your business. Hiring people can pay off limitless times and it could lead to a return of thousands and thousands of dollars.

I'm not trying to beat anybody up over this topic, but if you look at it logically, then you realize that you must invest in your business to get the highest possible return. Wealth just doesn't come by socking away money in the bank and waiting for a return, especially at today's savings rates.

AN INVESTMENT COMPARISON:

Let's compare two ways of investing—one in a rental property and the other in your business.

If you invest in a $100,000 rental house and your mortgage payment on that house is $600 per month, you could generate a positive cash flow of $100 per month by charging $700 per month for the rent. This scenario assumes you have some cash for a down payment and you're OK with all the headaches of being a landlord. Are you also OK with the time and expense to make repairs and for maintenance? Having to find new tenants? Repairing a roof? And on and on it goes with managing rental properties.

Contrast that with investing $100 each week in a newspaper advertisement to grow your business.

To illustrate the comparison, draw a line down the center of your paper (See next page for drawing). Label the left-hand column "Rental House" and the right column "My Business." At the top of the left column write on the first line "House and $100,000." One line two write "Rent and $700 per month." On line three write "Mortgage Payment and $600." Subtract the $600 from the $700 and you get a net positive cash flow of $100 per month or $1,200 for the year. This is a very simplified example because we haven't considered taxes and insurance and other costs of owning a rental property. But let's do keep it simple.

Now in the "My Business" column let's start with "Newspaper Ads and $100 per week." Multiplying that by 52 weeks gives you an annual cost of $5,200 for the ads. Assume you get 20 responses each week on average. Sometimes it will be higher and sometimes lower. On the next line we multiply 20 times 52 weeks and you see you will have a total of 1,040 responses for the year from those ads.

Do you think you could find just one good producer out of those 1,040 people? Of course! Let's say you hire one person that can write $10,000 in personal issued paid production each month. Write $10,000 per month on the next line.

Let's say you have a 10-point spread with this person (you're at the 65% commission level and your new agent is at the 55% level). From that $10,000 per month producer you earn $1,000 per month, or $12,000 a year. That's if you only find one person that can do that. You've paid off your 12 month investment in five months! It's all gravy beyond that. Think of all the referrals you probably got on top of that. If that person keeps producing, you keep making a ROI long after the initial $5,200 for ads was paid off. And, you know you'll find more than one good producer out 1,040 responses to your ads! DO THE MATH!

THE POWER OF MONEY DIAGRAM

Rental House

House	$100,000

Per Month:

Rent	$700
Mortgage	$600
	$100

Net positive cash flow for the year:

	$100
	x 12 months
	$1,200

My Business

Newspaper Ads:

	$100/wk
	x52/wks
Annual Cost of Ads	$5,200/yr

Responses per week:

	20
	x 52/wks
	40
	100
Total Annual Responses	$1,040

Issued Paid Monthly Production:

	$10,000
	x 10%
	$1,000/month
	x 12 wks
From ONE Producer	$12,000/yr

WHICH INVESTMENT WOULD YOU RATHER MAKE?

Do you want the investment that can keep paying you off with bigger and bigger spreads or the one where you get the phone call at 10 p.m. on a Saturday evening that the toilet doesn't work?

It literally pays to become financially literate. Learn how money works. Be smart with your money and make it grow exponentially! More about money…

Two Categories of Money in your Life: Assets and Liabilities

Increase your assets and decrease your liabilities: that's basic economics.

True assets make you money—new assets—and do not hurt your bottom line

The "broke-minded" people think that their home and their car are assets. They're not! It takes money to run a car and it takes money to keep a home in proper order. That car loses value every day you own it. Rental properties are liabilities. Assets create for you, liabilities take away.

When I make a sale, get a referral, or get an agent writing business, it becomes an asset for me. I take some of the money from the sale and use it to find more good people to work with, I invest in more staff to help me do more work, or I help more agents make a sale to get them rolling.

Maybe I decide to buy a $100 lead. If I make a sale and get five referrals, then that was well worth $100. Those would all be considered assets for me. I'm using those things to create more ROI (Return On Investment) down the road.

Examples of finding ASSETS in our business —creates income for you:

- An agent that consistently produces every month
- A builder finds a builder that finds a builder, and keeps building a huge hierarchy

Examples of Liabilities—what you don't want! —Takes away income from you.

- Your house shouldn't be a liability, but it is a tremendous liability. You have electricity, cable, lawn care, and property taxes. All this hurts you every day, month, and year. It's a liability.

- An agent with a poor care ratio is also a liability. Care ratio is the number of issued paid applications divided by the number of A-leads allocated to you in a specific time period. For example, if an agent purchases 20 A-leads and gets only one sale, uh oh! That's not good. What did that cost you? I'm guessing you lost money on that deal!

- A builder that teaches anything other than the basics is dangerous.

TRUE ASSETS CREATE ADDITIONAL ASSETS

When you have true assets, they create additional assets for you, and they do not create liabilities. The sooner you learn this, the better off you will be. Follow the basics that help you create assets and avoid liabilities. Rental properties are a great example of this. It is hard to cash flow enough to make a good ROI when it comes to real estate. You can do it, but it's not easy. Kiyosaki gives excellent examples of this in two of his great business books that all agents should read: *Rich Dad, Poor Dad* and *Cashflow Quadrant*.

MISCONCEPTIONS OF MONEY

- You can save your way to wealth
- T.V./Radio "Money Personalities" are always knowledgeable in creating wealth
- Spending money to make money is bad
- Assets are something you own with stationary value

THE DYNAMIC OF THE BASE

The mighty oak tree is a great example of the base you are building. A tree can grow strong with a massive root structure. You (your organization) are the tree in this picture, with great branches and roots. So think about that healthy root system. If it's deep and it's wide, and you lose a root, you won't lose the tree. In this example below, if you lose D, your root structure can still go down with A, B, C, and E. And you can still work with D1, D2, D3 and D4, too. So, the idea is to have a healthy base, and the deeper you go and the wider you go, the more your tree is going to bear fruit. That fruit being the revenue, that fruit being the time that comes back to you, that fruit being a joyous life, a life full of production, and a life full of results. The life you design.

DRAWING YOUR TEAM OUT DIAGRAM

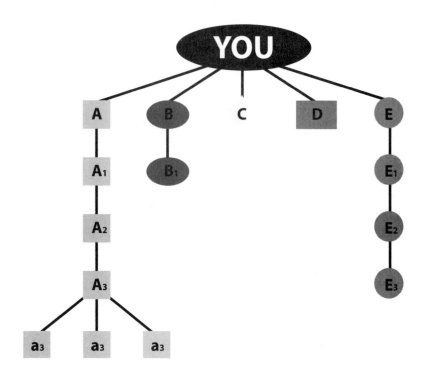

BUILDING DEPTH

The concept of building deep is one of security with a backup plan. You might think it is unusual to build a backup plan in the very beginning, but that's just like carrying a spare tire. You may not need it when your car is new, but you have it for a backup, should you have a flat. It's like life insurance. People say the unexpected happens. It IS going to happen; it should be expected. You should prepare. Building depth is your backup plan.

Therefore, the first statement on going deep is: if you have an agent, you have to find another agent underneath that agent. As a matter of fact, we say you don't have an agent until that agent has an agent. That is what moves you up to our second level, Business Developer.

BUSINESS DEVELOPER STRUCTURE

In our organization each individual hierarchy that we build we refer to as a "leg." If you only have one agent, you haven't started a leg. You only have a nub. It only becomes a leg when you have multiple people in it, and multiple people are selling. The statistical model says you'll have one good person as you go down four levels…under A you have B, C, D.

BUILDING DEPTH VERTICAL DIAGRAM

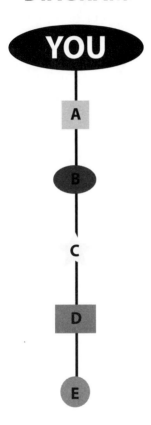

Typically, you will have one person in the four who is going to stand out (one who is "moving") quite a bit more than the other three. That's your person! That's the one you will focus on and help first.

So, our version of a solid leg occurs when it's at least four deep and you have identified the one person out of the four that will duplicate and copy what you do. Often times, when you hire an agent, they will quit for one reason or another. Often times, people stay for one reason or another. If they stay, it's all good. You have helped them start a business. If they quit, you still have at least one backup (like your spare tire), maybe multiple backups under that agent in that particular leg/hierarchy.

If you were to go four wide, the same thing happens. So depth can be viewed by twisting your paper sideways and saying this is the same four.

BUILDING DEPTH HORIZONTALLY DIAGRAM

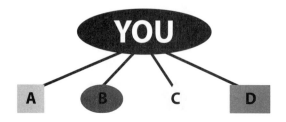

You're still working in depth. When you help A do this, he now has a terrific reason to stay in the business with you. It's called hope of making money through an organization that is being built underneath him. He sees a chance. He sees potential. People are always willing to pay more and faster for future money, future potential, and a better tomorrow. Everyone wants to believe that tomorrow is better, and in this agent's case, because you're working with him in depth; his tomorrow is brighter than his current situation. He wants to be around for that party.

By taking this first agent you've hired out four wide at minimum (it could be six wide, it could be three wide, but the goal is four wide MINIMUM), you've helped yourself go deeper. Because your agent A has four wide, there is one of the four with more potential for you to drop down and go deeper. The best person you find under agent A is the one you should work with to try to build the depth under. It's easier than trying to drag someone along. Just as if you were digging a hole in your yard, you don't want to dig where there is rock. You want to go where there's soft ground and you can dig easily. A good place to put your focus is on people who have had successes in their life already. That's the person who will probably have the better list, and people will be more receptive to their leadership. It's your job to drop down under this agent, the best of the four, let's call him the star—a small star since it's only out of a few people. Your role here is to take this small star and drop down and help him become four wide, and from that four you drop down to another four. The concept is to go four, drop down four, drop down four, drop down four, and drop down four so that you get four deep.

GET FOUR DEEP DIAGRAM

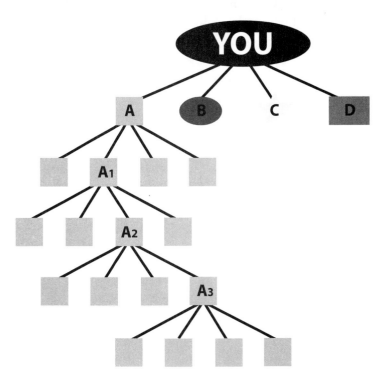

Now, you're looking for someone back up at the top, like B, to drop down and copy you. We call this working around, and working through, when you go down to D and you take B with you. You go down to G and you take C with you. They ride with you, they talk with you, and they understand the concepts. You're teaching them how to build depth.

That's when momentum kicks in, and keep in mind that momentum is built by personal production, then it goes to organizational momentum, then it leads to people winning. So in this concept, once you get down to J, you look back up and you look at who is winning. For example, B is starting to copy you—he's actually working in his second leg getting it four wide. Maybe he's even working his third leg and helping get it four wide. The agent who duplicates you in his third and fourth legs is the person you really want to start to work with to build a long-term relationship.

YOU WORKING WITH DOWNLINES DIAGRAM

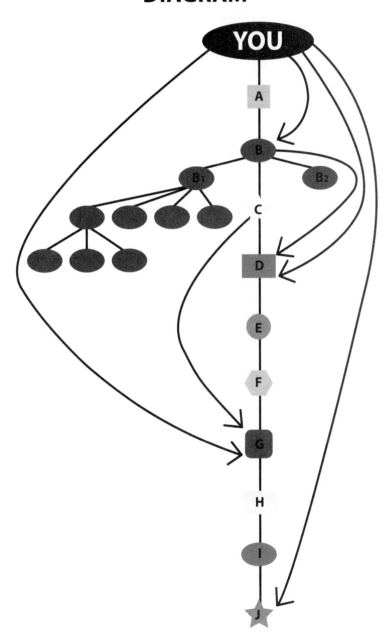

Often times you will drop down to A, and drop down to B, and drop down to C, and you might work with C building two legs, or two organizations, and start dropping them down, but you won't do much more than two for any agent. So if that agent goes out and does the same thing in legs three and four, that's the agent who is really starting to become a bigger star in your organization because he's taken personal responsibility that is creating organizational momentum. That's when people begin to win, and then the individual winners' momentum starts to really kick in.

As you look at the levels, a lot of credibility is gained when you move up to Team Leader. For Team Leader you must have six agents under you. You have helped at least four legs start writing business, and you have depth writing business in at least two legs.

YOU WORKING WITH DOWNLINES 2 DIAGRAM

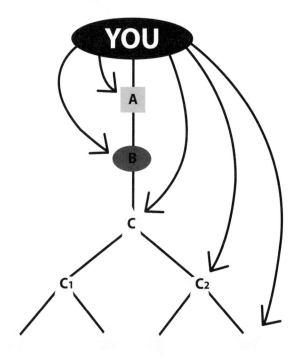

The program starts to get serious, and you make the "big money" when you get up to the Agency Leader level where you must have two solid legs. Two solid legs.

AGENCY LEADER STRUCTURE

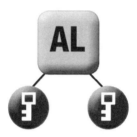

Then, the next step is to Key Agency Leader. Now you're helping others get their head start toward Agency Leader.

KEY AGENCY LEADER STRUCTURE

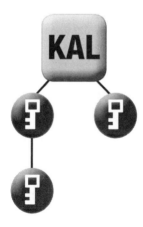

When you move up to MVP you're really becoming a star because you have the ability to build that third leg on your own. At this point there's no stopping you!

MVP AGENCY LEADER STRUCTURE

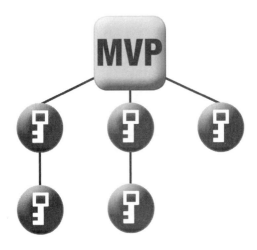

SO, KEEPING IT SIMPLE:

- Start four wide
- Go deep—drop down to the stand-out person
- Get that person four wide
- Do it again
- Do it again
- Do it again
- You're working to get 12 deep (See following page for diagram)

When you get 12 deep you'll have at least four great people. You'll have an awesome team structure with three or four agents ready to go to Key Leader, and you now have the unlimited income potential that National Agents Alliance provides those who will do the work and follow the system!

YOUR DEPTH DIAGRAM

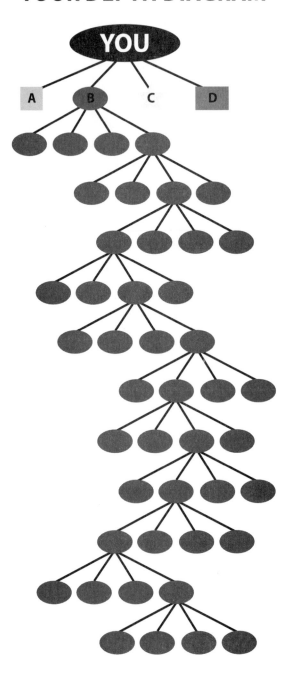

THE POWER OF NAACTIVITY

The NAActivity book is the agent's most essential tool for keeping track of the daily activities that will determine success or failure in this business. It's like a super, hyped-up Stephen Covey day planner on steroids. We know Covey's is more sophisticated, so we've really broken it down for our agents.

It has been designed for simplicity, and really works for the agent, if the agent works. If you can master the mundane, the simplest day-to-day tasks that you must do to create the big dreams you have for you and your family, and properly use the NAActivity book to track those simple tasks, you will master the system that has produced some of the highest paid agents in the entire industry.

With the NAActivity book open, you can see across the top of the left-hand page the four columns for tracking DIALS, CONTACTS, APPOINTMENTS, and APPLICATIONS. Starting with the DIALS column, we keep it really simple: every time you dial a number, you put a mark in the column (see example below). For our purposes, a dial occurs when you punch in enough numbers on your phone to make it ring on the other end. It doesn't matter whether you get an answering machine or a person answers—you dialed and it rang, that counts as a dial and you mark it down in the DIALS column. If you call back, it counts; if you call their cell number, it counts; if you call their work number, it counts. You call another prospect, it counts. On the fifth dial, make your mark crossways—this is what we call a "haystack" which makes it easier to count the total dials (see next page).

By breaking it down to its simplest form we can make sure that anybody can understand it and no one can deny knowing exactly what to do. Children use this excuse all the time—"I don't know what you mean." Some irresponsible agents might say, "I didn't know what you meant." So, by making it very simple it is crystal

NAACTIVITY SAMPLE PAGES

clear. There is no excuse. Plus, we make it easy to make a dial or get a point with the NAActivity book. Each time you make a dial, you get a mark in the DIALS column.

You can determine how long your dialing session will take by timing a call from the time you begin dialing until someone answers or you get the answering machine. Let's say that call takes 23 seconds. Your goal is to make 500 dials in a week, and each dial takes 23 seconds, so that's 500 times 23 and that equals 11,500 seconds. So divide that by 60 seconds and your dials will take 192 minutes or 3.2 hours. Now keep in mind, if a person answers the phone or you leave a message on the answering machine the call will take longer than 23 seconds. Another way you can determine your dialing time is to call for a solid hour and see how many dials you get completed. Now that's your standard. Or call for two hours, count the dials, divide by two, and that's how many calls you can make in an hour. An agent can look at the NAActivity book and check the numbers. Some agents will look at the numbers and make excuses for them not being better. They were cleaning their office, reading e-mails, or doing anything other than making dials. You have to ask, if that's your job, "what could be more important than making dials?"

Obviously, you will need to set aside time for running appointments. The reason for the first column is to keep it very simple so an agent cannot make excuses for activity. They CAN make excuses for not having the talent to book an appointment. They CAN make excuses for not closing the sale at the appointment, but they CAN NOT make an excuse for the activity part. It's like when your dad says, "you've got to go to work" and you might say, "but I can't do the job" and that might be true. You might not have the talent or the skill level. It's the showing up at work that anybody can do. The NAActivity book is all about the "showing up" part of our business. All you have to do is press the numbers on the phone. If you fail because you don't have talent, skill, or knowledge, that's different than not showing up. This gets it down to the very rudimentary, simplest steps that anybody can do... show up for work, make the dials, and record your dials. Skills will improve, results will improve, IF you just show up.

What's great about the NAActivity book is you can see exactly what you're doing, and your Manager (or your spouse, for that matter) can look at the DIALS column and see if you are working. This DIALS column tells the story. It's not the number of times someone says "hello." It's the number of times that someone answers that will go in the CONTACTS column. If you make an appointment, that goes in the APPOINTMENTS column. You can't control people saying "hello," but you CAN control the dials. Skill takes over when someone says "hello" and you set the appointment, but the dials...anybody can do.

The number of contacts is a function of the dials. Setting the appointment and making the sale is where the skills kick in. A lot of agents set their goals around skills...setting the appointment and closing the sale. So now, they can come up with an excuse, but you can't have an excuse for dialing. Some agents will make 250 calls, some will call 500. Whether it's 100 or 600 we have to evaluate the results. If you only set four appointments all week, and in the DIALS column there are only 50 dials, the question you have to ask is "Why only 50? If I only have four appointments, shouldn't I be making more calls?"

What is the reason?

Is it fear?

We don't acknowledge fear of dialing. You just press the numbers on the phone; they can't come through the phone and do anything to you. This, again, is the showing up part.

Another determining factor in these numbers is whether or not the agent has enough leads, contacts, or referrals to make the dials. That's why NAA has the TLP leads that are just 10 cents each, and most Managers will supply them to their agents at no cost. There really is no excuse to have low numbers in the DIALS column.

Let's use the numbers another way. If you make $5,000 in a week and you made 400 dials, you can say you made $12.50 per dial ($5,000 divided by 400 = $12.50). So for every time you take 23 seconds to dial a number you make $12.50 (See diagram on next page). How great is that! So you can see how you can calculate how much you'll make per dial. So, here's another example. Let's say you make $4 for every dial you make. The question is, "how much money do you want to make?" If you want to make $1,500 per week, divide $1,500 by $4 and you see you need to make 375 phone calls to produce enough appointments to net enough applications to earn the $1,500 in commissions. It's that simple. The NAActivity book will track your results. At your current skill level you can determine how much you can earn per dial. This will show you how your work level ties to your skill level. To increase your income, increase your work level. If your current skill level equates to $4 per dial, and you earn that $1,500 on 375 dials, but you want to earn $2,000...divide $2,000 by $4 and you get 500. There it is! Just increase your dials from 375 to 500!

NUMBERS INTO PERSPECTIVE DIAGRAM

$5,000 per week /400 dials = $12.50 per dial

Remember, there's a time element involved here. Recall how we calculate how long it will take to make 300, 500, or 700 calls and factor in the time it takes to run the appointments and write the applications. The way to take the lid off the time factor is to recruit other agents, so you can leverage your time (this will be discussed in a subsequent section). However, keep in mind, your skill level is in between the money you earn and the number of dials you make. Everyone tries to compare skill levels between agents, but what is your work level compared to the other agent? What it really comes down to is, what is the best YOU can do in dials and what's the best dollars per dial you can create?

Your NAActivity book reflects your results. When you total up your dials at the end of the week you could put that number in a little box. That number says exactly what your work level was for the week. Stories don't fit in the box. Excuses won't fit in the box. Life's drama doesn't fit in the box. Here's what matters: HOW MANY DIALS DID YOU MAKE?

At the end of the week your numbers will look something like this:

400 DIALS led to 100 CONTACTS that led to 20 APPOINTMENTS that led to 14 APPLICATIONS (see following page).

With the activity numbers posted on this page, the Agency Manager can judge the skill level of the agent and determine just what training will help that agent improve. NAA makes available to all agents a huge array of books and MP3s recorded by some of the industry's top producers. Most importantly, NAA provides opportunities to associate with trainers that have excellent skills and experience, and the willingness to mentor the new agent. NAA considers personal development through reading, listening, and association to be absolutely ESSENTIAL to success in this business, and these activities MUST be scheduled EVERY DAY just like the activities tracked in the NAActivity book.

WEEKLY NAACTIVITY NUMBERS EXAMPLE

	Dials			Contacts	Appointments	Applications
Friday	(tally marks)			(tally marks)	III	II
Saturday	(tally marks)			(tally marks)		
Sunday	(tally marks)			(tally marks)		
Monday	(tally marks)			(tally marks)	I IIIII	IIIII
Tuesday	(tally marks)			(tally marks)	IIIII I	I II
Wednesday	(tally marks)			(tally marks)	II	II
Thursday	(tally marks)			(tally marks)	III	II
TOTAL			*400*	*100*	*10*	*14*

Earlier, we mentioned leveraging your time by recruiting other agents and building your own agency. With that in mind, let's take a look at the column headings across the top of the right hand page in the NAActivity book. You'll see RECRUITING DIALS, S.T.P., FASTRACKS, AND AGENTS CONTRACTED.

Just as you did on the left-hand page in tracking your dials to client prospects, you'll use the first column on the right-hand page to track your dials to prospective recruits, your future business partners. You will use newspaper ads, www.CareerBuilder.com ads, www.Craigslist.com ads, and your warm-market list, plus referrals to insure a never-ending supply of possible recruits for your business-building dials.

This activity is crucial to your future development of passive, residual income, and time must be budgeted for these dials just as you did with calling client prospects. With assistance from your Agency Manager, the new agent will be taught the skills necessary to set the all-important appointments that we track in the second column, S.T.P…SHOW THE PLAN.

The S.T.P. appointments will be set as a face-to-face, a webinar, or a group presentation at a weekly HotSpots briefing conducted by NAA leaders at hotel meeting rooms or agent's offices. By utilizing the weekly HotSpots a new agent can bring multiple guests to see an experienced, expert agent leader SHOW THE PLAN, and have the guests meet top NAA producers.

In the third column, FasTracts, the agent places a mark for every prospective recruit that makes the decision to join the business and start the process by registering for an agent number at the recruiting agent's NAA website. If not already licensed, the new FasTract agent will now begin the process to obtain a Life and Health Insurance license through their state insurance department. If already licensed, the new agent begins on-the-job training immediately, working with the sponsoring agent and upline Agency Manager to rapidly start the NAActivity that will lead to that first commission check!

The final column on this page, AGENTS CONTRACTED, is used to track those new agents who have completed the contracting process with each of our insurance carriers that allows the agent to write business with that company.

The secret to the NAActivity book is to use it. It's simple and easy to do. It's also easy not to do. The successful agent applies the simple, daily disciplines that seem so small and insignificant, but when done consistently every single day, add up to a huge, ever-growing business with absolutely no limits on its potential. As Ralph Waldo Emerson said, "Do the thing and you will have the power. But they that do not the thing, had not the power." The NAActivity system is designed to insure your success. JUST DO IT!

GETTING REFERRALS

Referral leads are definitely out there, and in this chapter we will tackle how to help you unearth what is already available and teach you what to say and what to do when you go into a client's home.

We have had people take one A-lead and use it to explode their business. There have been cases where by closing one lead, the agent has then snagged 30 referrals and sold 27 more policies to clients. That's just one example.

WHAT IS THE GOAL FOR REFERRALS?

The goal is to get at least 10 referrals in every home we visit. That's the minimum number you should collect before you leave a home. There is no reason you can't leave with 25 or 30, but at least get 10 or you are just not trying hard enough.

When you start getting a list of referrals, try to draw it out like you would your group or team. Draw it out wide, and draw it out in depth too.

Your mindset should be to protect the ENTIRE family by getting a warm-market list from the client you just sold. It should be your mission to protect the client you are with, but also to help protect their immediate family, their extended family, and their friends. It begins with having an attitude that you care enough about them to go above and beyond what most people would to make sure the people they care about are taken care of should the unexpected happen. It's a serve-and-protect mentality.

In this business, our agents must care about helping people. If you truly care and provide good service to the client, the commissions will take care of themselves. The more you serve, the more rewards will come your way. The referrals are just another avenue to reach people that otherwise probably would not purchase life insurance because they just don't know what is available to them. Ask for those referrals!

In Richard Fenton's Go For No, he talks about not stopping when a client tells you no the first time you ask. If you don't ask five times and get a no five times, then you have not tried hard enough. If you don't value the client enough to keep asking, then you don't care enough.

Once you have finished wrapping up the original reason you came to the client's home, you want to talk to them about creating a list. Do this at the end or close to the end of your visit.

3 Ways to Get Referrals

- Emergency Response System
- RX brochures
- Straight referrals

EMERGENCY RESPONSE SYSTEM STORY

The first way to get a list of referrals is to talk to the client about a story of a person dying and the insurance company not paying out for two months. It's not that they didn't want to pay off the policy, but the person who died had hidden the paperwork and it couldn't be located. It might be in a drawer somewhere, a safe or even under a mattress. We offer a service to eliminate that potential with them. By providing a list of people who can contact us should something happen to the client; you are going to expedite the process of helping the insurance carrier pay off the policy. Start by asking for a list of 10 people that are responsible enough to contact you should the client pass away. The spouse or other close family member may be too distraught during this grieving time to remember what needs to be done. That's why we help the client pick out at least 10 sharp people who they trust to handle that responsibility. The chances are very high that at least one of those

10 will get in touch with you in the event that the client should die. Our clients love this service and willingly give a long list of reliable people to contact. Our attitude and our approach is not "do you want to do this?" The attitude is "the last thing we ARE going to do is put this list in place."

Just flip over the application and simply write ERS at the top of the page. Ask the client who they want at the top of the list. Once you get the first name, keep your head down, and don't make a lot of eye contact. Get the name, relationship to the client, phone number, and where they live (city and state they live in is enough; you don't have to get an exact address). Once you get one name and the information, ask "who is next?" Keep going. If they get stuck, suggest a friend. Suggest a co-worker. Keep asking! If they make excuses, keep pressing. Wait if you have to, but keep asking, "Who is next?" Ask the client, "If I could squeeze a few more names on the list, who would they be?" Keep growing the list until they are just adamant that they are out of names.

Example:

ERS

Name	Relationship	#	City
1.			
2.			
3.			
4.			
5.			
6.			
7.			
8.			
9.			
10.			
11.			
12.			

Don't stop at 10 or 12. Make the list as long as the client wants it to be! This is another way to show the client that you care about them and you want to make sure their family will be taken care of should they die. If they want to stop at three or four, tell them, "I have to have 10." Be confident, have a strong posture. You are providing a great service to this client.

USING RX BROCHURES

One of the great additions to our marketing program in the last year that really helps the client save money and gets us referrals is the Rx brochure. These cards are free for our clients and they help people save insane amounts of money on their medical prescriptions. These cards save our clients around an average of 26 percent on over the counter drugs, eye glasses, mobility aides, prescription medicine, etc…We allow each client to give away six of these cards to friends and family after they purchase a policy with one of our carriers.

When we offer this Rx brochure, we once again show that we care about helping their family save money, and we get another list of people to visit.

We have found that these Rx brochures are very popular and have saved people hundreds of dollars monthly. Diabetics, for example, get a large discount on their medicine using our Rx brochures, and clients using blood pressure medicine, cholesterol medicine, migraine medicine (Topamax), etc…all benefit as well.

A batch of 50 Rx brochures can be purchased very inexpensively through www.ShopAtNAA.com. NOTE: The cards are free if printed off the Internet at www.NAARxCard.com. If you sell one policy using the Rx brochures, you will make a big return over the cost of buying a pack of 50 of these brochures.

Emergency Response System™ Form (Lead)

Enter the Emergency Contacts from this application and submit with your paperwork.
Your ERS™ letters will be sent out to the contacts on your behalf automatically,
using the information in your NAA® profile.

Emergency Contact -

Name:

Cell Phone: Work Phone:

Address:

City:

State: Zipcode: Home Phone:

Email:

Emergency Contact for:
(enter applicant's name as it should appear on ERS™ letter)

Emergency Contact -

Name:

Cell Phone: Work Phone:

Address:

City:

State: Zipcode: Home Phone:

Email:

Emergency Contact for:
(enter applicant's name as it should appear on ERS™ letter)

Emergency Contact -

Name:

Cell Phone: Work Phone:

Address:

City:

State: Zipcode: Home Phone:

Email:

Emergency Contact for:
(enter applicant's name as it should appear on ERS™ letter)

000000   LER

HANDLING REFERRALS

After you get the ERS list, or names from Rx cards, you want to ask the client how many people on that list would be interested in getting some information about what we do. One effective way is to nod at them and say, "I bet all of them might be interested in what we offer our clients."

The RX brochure allows your client to have a personal RX Card to keep in their wallets so that they are easy to find.

If you are selling three or four policies a week, you are likely to end up with around 50 referrals. This is a good problem to have. Ask the client who are the most likely three or four people from the list who could use our services. These people are likely married with kids. As they rattle off the four or five most likely, make a notation beside those names and ask for permission to contact those people. You should emphasize the fact that your client could greatly impact the life of another person and an entire family by just referring them to you. It is especially important for those people with children. When you put it in that perspective, they are going to likely point out a handful of people because those are the people they care about most. This is an area where emotion is a very important element that is in play.

Before you realize it, you've got a fresh list of people to contact by asking simple questions. Before you even get back to your office or home, you can start calling the people on your new referral list!

With this extra list of names and numbers you can supplement the minimum 250 dials you are making weekly. These people are not a replacement for the leads system, they are a supplement, and

	Emergency Response System / Follow Up			Agent: John Smith NAA123456					

Client		Spouse/Other	Date	Co/plan					

#	Name	Relationship	Phone #	Address	Ben	ERS	Rx	Ref	STP
1									
2									
3									
4									
5									
6									
7									
8									
9									
10									
11									
12									
13									
14									
15									
16									
17									
18									
19									
20									

they are FREE. Keep in mind that these names are not qualified leads yet. You need to call each person and work your referral phone script, working off the credibility of the client who gladly provided the name.

EXAMPLE OF REFERRAL PHONE SCRIPT:

Hey _____! How are you doing? You don't know me, but I actually sat down with _____ on _____. My name is _____. Did _____ give you a call and let you know that I was going to call? (Yes or No)

I actually was working with _____ to help set up his family in the event that something happened to _____, so the family would be protected. _____ listed you as an emergency contact on that policy, so he's asking that you do that for _____. Are you willing to do that? (Yes or No)

What we did for _____ is set up a program that will pay off their house if something happened to _____. What we're asking you to do is call us if, God forbid, something were to happen to _____. If that were to happen you would definitely need to call us, does that make sense? (Yes or No)

Also, if _____ were to get sick, get hurt at work or something like that and can't work, I'm guessing _____ will call us. However, would you mind giving us a courtesy call just in case, so we can make sure _____ can keep up with bills, mortgage, etc...? (Yes or No)

Really quick, let me give you my information (Phone Number here), and this is the company we set this up with (Mutual of Omaha, ING, Foresters, etc.) and their number is (Phone number here). If anything happens, please let us know.

They gave me your number as the emergency contact, but they also told me that you would be an ideal candidate to benefit from getting some type of coverage like this set up for your family. Is this true (INSERT NAME HERE) _____? (Yes or No)

IF YES...You live over in (CITY or AREA GOES HERE) _____, right? (Yes or No)

I'll be in that area on (Day) helping some other families, so what I can do is swing by at around (Pick a time). Does that work for you? (Yes or No)

IF you get a NO, tell them no problem, but please call us if something happens to _____. If something changes with them, please also feel free to call us.

IF you get a YES, then you repeat the day and time you are coming and end the conversation with some small talk.

During this conversation, you have actually gotten this person interested in some of the benefits of the products we offer without selling over the phone. This gives the person a little better idea of what the product can do for them. You are not talking about terms or exact numbers. This is just a neat way to tie it all back together, and from there you can make an appointment to take them product information. You are not trying to force anything with these calls, but you are offering to meet with them if that is something that would interest them. There is no need to press them to meet with you. You have already met with a family member or friend. If they need our service, they will meet with you and it will be the easiest sale you can make.

When you get in the home, use small talk to ease into a conversation about why they think it is important for their family to be protected. Let them verbally tell you their why, even if you think you know what it is. We are "need identifiers" and "problem solvers."

UNDERSTANDING HUMAN NATURE

THE ALBRIGHT ZONE

93% < 7% Content

38% Voice

55% Body Language

WHAT COMMUNICATES TO PEOPLE?

- Recruit people to an environment/ atmosphere of winning—no logic
- People will respond to what they feel not hear.
- We build people and also sell products

STAR QUALITY

We all know some people that seem to have the "IT" factor that separates them from "Joe Common." What is "IT?" How did they get this? Were they born with it? Did somebody teach them how to be this way?

My guess is they were not born this way, even though your upbringing certainly can play a role in shaping this trait. Even if a person is born with something special in them, they still have to develop their "Star Qualities," and the biggest factor in star quality is charisma. The level of charisma can be cultivated and refined through association with other "stars," those high-producing leaders who have already put NAA on the map, earned the big dollars, and paved the way for those willing to follow. It's like when you were a kid, and your parents told you not to associate with a certain crowd because you'd surely start picking up all their bad ways, that you should find some better friends to hang with. Well, if you want to be a millionaire, we say, "don't hang out with dollar-aires." Associate with winners. Anyone can learn the "content" part of our business; we want our new agents to develop into "stars." Hang with the "stars" so you get the other 93 percent that they communicate through their body language, the command of their voice, their "charisma"—the "IT" they display that acts like a magnet as they attract friends, followers, and lots of money.

CHARISMA

According to the 2010 version of the New Oxford American dictionary, charisma is defined as a compelling attractiveness or charm that can inspire devotion in others, or a divinely conferred power or talent. The word charisma is Greek in origin and translates to "gift of divine grace."

- Charisma CAN be cultivated
- Some people just have a charismatic spark to them
- Charisma is powerful and it is almost like having magic powers
- Charisma in a leader is like a magnet that draws people in
- Nothing is more powerful than a charismatic leader who unifies a team
- Successful corporations typically have an inspiring, charismatic leader who pushes people to get involved, dream big, and understand the company vision and mission

- Charismatic leaders have the ability to plant seeds—or ideas—and watch others implement and grow the idea as if it were their own

- A person that is empowered with charisma can do the same for other people too, and this can lead to people doing more than they ever thought possible

When I communicate to our people I don't beat around the bush. I'm deliberate and direct. I care about all our people, and I want what's best for them, so I sometimes have to tell them things they might not want to hear. In fact, all our leaders "tell it like it is." If we didn't, we wouldn't be doing our job. We want to train a team of agents that will be aggressive and courageous, a team that will not accept failure, a team that will not accept the status quo, and a team that will get back up when they've been knocked down.

If we look to the leaders who built our great country, leaders who built gigantic business enterprises, even the leaders in sports that so many Americans admire and follow, you see common personal traits and skills now being taught in the military academies and the best business schools throughout the world.

Our founding fathers designed the greatest system in the history of mankind, and because of leaders like George Washington, Abraham Lincoln, Dr. Martin Luther King Jr., Dwight Eisenhower, General Norman Schwarzkopf, Notre Dame football coach Knute Rockne, Andrew Carnegie, John D. Rockefeller, and many others, we have had instilled in us a strong sense of patriotism and loyalty, and a belief that anything is possible. We have, to guide us, the wisdom of all the great leaders and entrepreneurs who have preceded us. It is our choice whether to use that wisdom for greater achievement and to understand that "thoughts become things," and "if man can dream it, he can achieve it." At NAA, we choose to think big and dream big, reach for the stars, achieve financial freedom, and make a difference in the lives of everyone we encounter.

I recently read the famous speech given by General George Patton to the 3rd Army and I found that it illustrates so well the importance of commitment and leadership in everything we do. If you want to read the uncensored version, you can find the entire speech on the internet, but you are forewarned about General Patton's strong language. Profanity is the language of soldiers, not most business leaders, but I want you to understand the important theme.

So here is the setting. This speech took place in a secret location in England on June 5, 1944, and was given to the 3rd Army, an infantry division preparing to race across Europe to destroy Germany's Adolph Hitler and his troops. His audience, the 3rd Army, is a mix of veteran soldiers and some young men facing their first taste of combat, all with worried family at home. Patton told the soldiers they could not mention in letters to their loved ones that he was there. No one was to know where the general was. This address has been called Patton's "Blood and Guts" speech and it really got me thinking about commitment, passion, and vision in leadership. Read the entire speech at historyinfilm.com/patton/bio, but here are a few small excerpts:

"…All through your Army careers, you men have bitched about … drilling. That, like everything else in this Army, has a definite purpose. That purpose is alertness. Alertness must be bred into every soldier… There are 400 neatly marked graves somewhere in Sicily all because one man went to sleep on the job. But they are German graves, because we caught the bastard asleep before they did. An army is a team. It lives, sleeps, eats, and fights as a team…

…My men don't surrender. I don't want to hear of any soldier under my command being captured unless he has been hit. Even if you are hit, you can still fight back… The kind of man that I want in my command is just like the lieutenant in Libya, who, with a Luger against his chest, jerked off his helmet, swept the gun aside with one hand, and busted the hell out of the Kraut with his helmet. Then he jumped on the gun and went out and killed another German before they knew what the hell was coming off. And, all of that time, this man had a bullet through a lung. There was a real man!

...All of the real heroes are not storybook combat fighters, either. Every single man in this Army plays a vital role. Don't ever let up. Don't ever think that your job is unimportant. Every man has a job to do and he must do it. Every man is a vital link in the great chain. What if every truck driver suddenly decided that he didn't like the whine of those shells overhead, turned yellow, and jumped headlong into a ditch? He could say, 'Hell, they won't miss me, just one man in thousands.' But, what if every man thought that way? Where in hell would we be now?... The ordinance men are needed to supply the guns and machinery of war to keep us rolling..."

If you read the speech, or even just parts of it, you'll see a leader, like all successful leaders, with conviction and commitment. Did Patton have "IT?" Did he have the charisma of a leader? Did he accept the status quo? Do you think he considered losing as an option? I don't think he ever considered second place as an option and he wouldn't let his men think that way either.

From this one speech, you can learn a lot about one of our greatest military leaders and the qualities that make a leader, whether for war or to use to build your business.

He communicated his vision (how they would win the war), he stressed the importance of every single soldier doing his part (teamwork) and showing up for work (no resting in foxholes, no weekends off), and he inspired loyalty from young American soldiers while he impressed upon them a fanatical sense of duty. Patton, like all great leaders, is never willing to settle for average and ordinary. Losers settle for average.

The point of all this is: NAA is just as serious about our mission as Patton was his. We have to protect our clients' families. We have to wipe out financial poverty and create a better life for our agents and their families. We have to develop leaders and build a huge team to go out and serve the masses. We have to identify the best and work with them while we weed out the weak. It may take a lot of blood, guts, and sweat to get to the top, but the rewards are worth the effort.

NAA is a company that has "IT." We have the great leaders with "charisma" and the environment and atmosphere where new agents can grow and develop. As Tim Goad has said, "People don't grow into leadership through information; they grow into great leaders through association and culture." That's right on, and definitely describes NAA. We live and teach the motto: Have Fun, Make Money, Make a Difference. Our culture creates and demands loyalty, and we have, like Patton, a bold, fanatical faith in our mission and a devotion to strong core values.

NASA CAN HELP MAN WALK ON THE MOON

People often assume that what they do does not make a difference. If everyone took a stance and truly thought their daily tasks—small or large—helped change the world, then the world would be different. No matter what you do, as long as you are doing something positive, YOU MATTER!

Tim Goad is one of my favorite people and one of his favorite sayings is: "You matter." At NAA, every single agent, every single client matters. You matter. You make a difference. You help. You contribute. You are part of a team that is going somewhere. You are part of a team that is having fun, making money, and making a difference in people's lives. I am reminded of a story of a reporter visiting NASA's Apollo program noticing a janitor working at a high rate of speed and with a sense of urgency about him. The reporter asked him how long he had worked there and he said for years. The reporter then asked him why he seemed to do things with such urgency. The janitor quickly told the reporter, "I'm cleaning up for the team that is going to put a man on the moon. It's urgent that we do it for our country and our team." The janitor stepped back and realized that a team had been created at NASA, and there was now not only a chance, but likelihood that NASA would put a man on the moon because everyone on the team mattered. Everyone cared. NASA started Oct. 1, 1958. On July 20, 1969, Neil Armstrong took man's first steps on the moon.

There are still those types of stories going on in America today. People still dream big, and they desire to be part of a

> *"That's one small step for man; one giant leap for mankind."*
>
> –Astronaut
> **Neil Armstrong**

team's success. There's a revitalization going on in this country and it's incredible what a team can do when everybody understands what each individual can do when they know that they matter.

It's that kind of thinking that can make all the difference in the world. If you share the common purpose of the team, then you are going to be more efficient in your daily tasks—whether small or large duties.

If you can find people with that kind of mentality, look out! If you can be a leader that gets people to believe that what they do matters, then it is going to be on like Donkey Kong.

OUR SYSTEM

"The road to success can take a detour. I tell people that I don't care if they came from Yale or jail it's what you do from today that counts."

–Andy Albright

SHOW THE PLAN

When you are ready to stand up in front of small or large groups, you will be asked to "Show The Plan" (STP) at opportunity meetings. This is not that difficult…if you follow the outline and steps that will be taught to you.

We've broken it down into six easy steps, each taking around 10 minutes to cover. You are going to speak for about an hour, which sounds like a long time, but once you get the delivery down, it isn't that long. Here's a rundown of the six steps:

STEP 1: INTRODUCE YOURSELF

In the first 10 minutes or so, you will tell your story. You are going to tell the audience your background and how you got involved with this opportunity.

This is your personal story where you establish your credibility and help people identify with you.

4 THINGS TO REMEMBER HERE

- Relate to people where you were when you found NAA
- Tell how your manager found you and helped you start and build your business
- Use this time to edify your upline and give them adequate recognition
- Learn a transition statement to take you to Step 2. Example: Here is what I found out, and now I'm going to explain it to you as best I can…

Let's use my story as an example. My introduction would go something like the following:

I'm a small-town boy from Union Ridge, North Carolina, who achieved financial and personal success through a company called National Agents Alliance. While building NAA, my wife, partners, friends, and I have been blessed to see other people become financially successful as well. My journey really started before my company even started, so let me back up about 40 years.

Growing up, my parents worked hard, but they had limited resources that probably kept them from knowing what the "good life" really is. I knew this from a young age and I was determined not to live my life that way. Don't get me wrong, my parents took care of me. I had food, clothing, a roof over my head, etc..., but I wanted more than that. They did teach me to believe I could do whatever I wanted in life, and I have carried that mindset with me since an early age.

When I was young, I worked a lot of different jobs. I worked in tobacco, raked pine needles, and raised goats. I always used my money to reinvest in whatever business I was in. I did that with the hope of increasing my production capacity. More productivity would equal more money. That's about all I knew.

While I always worked hard at whatever job I had, I was always asking questions with the hope of finding ways to get ahead.

I worked hard and made good enough grades to attend North Carolina State University, where I earned a degree in Textile Science in 1986. I chose N.C. State because it was an agricultural and mechanical school, and my parents loved N.C. State athletics. The Carolinas were rich in textile manufacturing back then, and I knew with my degree and work ethic I would get a good job with a good company.

I made a decent living, but I was miserable at work. I was working for somebody else and I knew I would never run the company, and that bothered me. To really be happy, I knew I had to take back control, and that would mean leaving my J-O-B!

The turning point came in January of 1990 when my wife was diagnosed with Hodgkin's disease (a form of cancer). We quickly found out what we needed to do to find her the best medical care, so that's what we did. It was during this time that I totally committed to achieving an income level where Jane would never have to work again.

I kept working at my textile job. All the while I was feverishly working on side jobs that I hoped would lead to me finding financial freedom and would let me quit my textile job (that would soon be headed overseas anyway).

When my wife's cancer went into remission, we were in better shape financially, and we had our first child Haleigh in 1994. In 1997, I decided to quit my job and move back into the home where I grew up.

Jane and I were determined to find a business that would set us up to be financially free and allow us unlimited opportunity. I tried all kinds of things, and finally my cousin told me how much money you could make in financial services.

I started looking at life insurance. I looked at the statistics and realized that the "Baby Boomers" were incredibly deficient in owning life insurance. There were millions and millions of people who needed it and did not have it! That is still true today!

I had my answer and I started putting together a team to create National Agents Alliance. Through the opportunity of selling life insurance, we are helping people, making money, and making a difference. It's been 10 years since we started and I couldn't be happier.

Jane is still healthy, we have two wonderful children—Haleigh and Spencer—and I have achieved financial freedom. It's what I dreamt about as a young boy. Now, that doesn't mean I'm satisfied. I will always strive for a better future. Work is too much fun now. It is fun for the company and our agents. What we do is too rewarding to stop. I wake up glad to be alive, and I am ready to get going!

That's just an example. Everybody's story is different. You basically want to tell the audience where you were in life, why you needed a change, and how you ended up with NAA.

STEP 2: BABY BOOMER OPPORTUNITY

After you tell your story, you are going to talk about the opportunity we offer. The world's biggest wealth transfer is about to go down over the next 18 years. More than 10,000 Baby Boomers are going to turn 65 every single day until the year 2030! They are one demographic that is underprotected at a time when they need to be covered most. It's a huge void that we are helping fill. You might also want to mention that more than $3 trillion has been transferred from Baby Boomers so far, and there's another $10 trillion that is coming down the pike. There are 78 million Baby Boomers (1946-1964). SHICKYBOOM!

The market opportunity is HUGE. Things we want you to remember here are:

- The baby boomer generation is our prime target
- Here are 78 million Baby Boomers
- On Jan.1, 2011 the first Baby Boomer turned 65
- Every single day, for the next 19 years, 10,000 Baby Boomers will turn 65
- According to AARP, 40% of Baby Boomers have no adequate retirement and will work "until they drop." They need insurance and they need retirement investments
- YOU are at the RIGHT place and the RIGHT time!

STEP 3: CREDIBILITY AND WEALTH OF CARRIERS

How do we do it? Next, talk about all the great insurance carriers that we work with. Talk about Mutual of Omaha, ING, etc. Most people have heard of Mutual of Omaha's Wild Kingdom shows on the Animal Planet channel. Basically, talk about the millions and billions our carriers have to back us. This will help the guests understand the level of credibility of NAA and the carriers. They may not know NAA, but the chances are good they have heard of our carriers. With the huge Baby Boomer market and the sound financial position of these highly rated insurance companies we have the opportunity to do two great things—protect families all across the USA and earn as much money as we want. The carriers desire for us to promote and sell their products and in return, reward us financially.

SOME OF OUR CARRIERS INCLUDE:

- CFG: a New York-based $1 billion-dollar company
- Mutual of Omaha: a $35 billion-dollar company who wants us selling more!
- Foresters: a non-profit $13.5 billion-dollar company
- ING: the largest carrier we work with is a $335 billion-dollar company

At this point in your talk elaborate on how ALL these companies are INVESTING IN US!!!

BEYOND THE MONEY YOU CAN EARN, THEY GIVE US:

- Incentive trips…Dream vacations to exotic resorts all over the globe!
- Recognition: the carriers know who we are (NAA) and call our top producers by name
- Exclusive product development geared toward NAA's mission!
- Exclusive trips for our top leaders!

STEP 4: LEADS SYSTEM

Unlike some companies, we have leads that people send us! Seriously. We have an internal mailing house that sends out 1.2 million pieces of mail each week to people that go through a major life event. If somebody buys a house, refinances a house, gets married, has a baby, or has a death in the family, then they are going to receive a piece of mail from us. They fill out a questionnaire and mail it back to us, asking us to call them. It doesn't get any better than that!

LEAD EXAMPLES

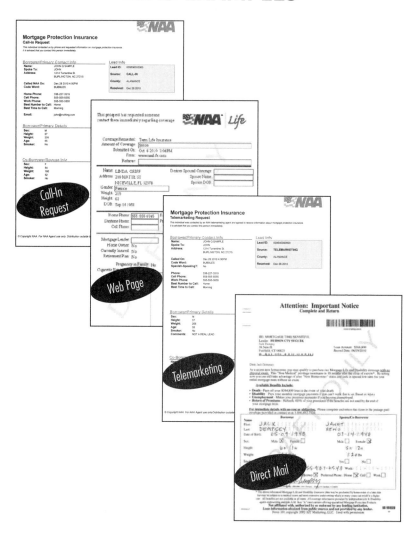

We focus our time on generating the best leads you can find anywhere. At this point in your talk, be sure to go over the different types of leads. Show examples of what our leads look like and what information you can find on them.

We take those leads and distribute them to our agents in all 50 states and they do the hard part. They pick up a telephone and call that prospect to help them get the protection they want.

Make sure you explain our power as a lead generator and marketing company, and that no one else does what we do!

Explain our direct mail campaign for:

- Mortgages
- Final expense
- Marriage mailings
- Divorce mailings
- Baby mailings
- Survivor mailings

We also have a telemarketing department! We have a setup using the Internet where you pay per click and it generates instant income. www.NAALife.com. This is INSTANT INCOME! It's not trial and error.

NAA has a system in place and a team that executes the game plan. We are not here to make friends; we are here to take over! We collect the leads, we organize them, and we deliver the leads to agents online, once they are ordered. The agent then calls the prospect who wants to be protected and they reach an agreement through our carriers. The clients get protected and our agents get paid! It's almost too easy. The best part of our system is that it is duplicatable.

At this point, talk to the potential agents about our system of recruiting and building a team of sharp people.

Explain in detail what it takes to become a Key Leader, and how this structure will get them on track to experience success in our industry.

KEY LEADER STRUCTURE

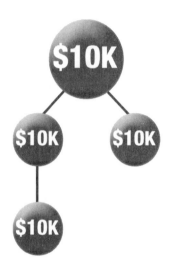

Draw out the Key Leader structure on the white board and show the commission split and profit examples! Do this for both personal and group examples. Bring up to the front of the room all KEY LEADERS and AGENCY MANAGERS so people can see what a KEY LEADER and an AGENCY MANAGER looks like!

STEP 5: DREAM BUILDING

Dream building is important. This is your opportunity to talk with the guests about dreams and goals. Everybody has a dream of some sort. Whether it's to pay off student loans, get out of debt, or just to have a little "extra" at the end of the month—everyone has a "why" as to their need of extra income. Share a small portion of your dream with the audience and personally relate some of your financial goals. Emphasize that in achieving dreams one will often go through struggles, meet adversity, and encounter road blocks—all of which will lead to victory if they "stay the course." This is the point in the meeting to sell NAA as a way to change the course of a person's life. NAA is a way to help other people while in return helping yourself.

STEP 6: THE 8 STEPS TO SUCCESS

One great way to close is to encourage the guest to read my book The 8 Steps to Success, especially if I'm there or coming soon. Promote that they can talk to me, meet me, get their book signed, and even get a picture with me if they'd like. I love when people approach me with questions and my book in their hand! This is a great way to have the guests catch the excitement NAA is generating all across North America and a great close to the meeting.

You have just finished your first meeting and you did it in about one hour! In review:

6 STEPS TO STP (AROUND 10 MINUTES EACH)

- Introduction of yourself and how you got involved
- Opportunity with the Baby Boomer market
- Credibility and wealth of carriers
- Leads system – sales and recruiting (Key Leader is big!)
- Dream building
- Selling 8 Steps to Success for 10 minutes is OK (Encourage everyone to book a follow up appointment: BAM-FAM!)

HOW TO SET UP A MEETING

Before you even think about holding a meeting, you have to know the proper way to set up a room and you need to have a number of things in place, organized, and taken care of well before an audience or speaker arrives. This involves having a checklist of things you have to do before you hold a meeting.

The next couple of pages will help teach you how to operate a successful meeting. It's a simple outline that we follow for all of our events. If followed correctly, people will remember it, and it will leave a lasting impression on their first impression of you and NAA. It's vital that you do this the right way.

You should use the checklist we have provided (Page 158-159) to ensure you are ready for your meeting. Make copies of it so you have it!

THERMOSTAT

The first thing you can do is crank up the Air Conditioning! Put the thermostat in the meeting room at 65 degrees or lower. If you can get it cooler, drop it down to 62! If you get a room full of people together, it will get warmer. It might even get hot.

LIGHTING

Lighting is important. The proper lighting can make or break a meeting too, regardless of the message a speaker delivers. First, you need to have bright lights! Make sure the power bill has been paid, so you have lights. It's important to make sure you don't have any bulbs burned out or any blinking lights. If you do, replace them or find someone to replace them for you! I'm not joking about this. You don't want the room too dim or to have flickering lights. Good lighting is important and you should make sure that it's taken care of right after you have started to cool the room down.

CHAIRS

You will need chairs. Don't show up and snap your fingers and say, "We need to find some chairs." Line that up with your hotel or your host. It sounds simple, but I've seen people having to scramble for chairs right before meetings. Don't let that happen to you. They should be clean chairs too. Check for stains, broken legs, broken seat backs, etc.

You want neat rows arranged with adequate spacing. You want a larger space in the middle that creates a walkway to the front where your speaker will be. Make your rows consistent. Make it neat. Make it professional. See DIAGRAM on page 157.

ENTRANCE

This is huge. People often ask the following: "I've got two doors, or three doors; which one(s) should people use to enter my meeting?" Great question. The entrance should always be at the back of the room. You don't want people entering from the front where the speaker is. People will show up late, and you don't want to embarrass them or your speaker by making them walk in front of everybody. It's disruptive to the audience and the speaker. Yes, they should have been early, but things happen. If you have two doors at the rear of a room, it's OK to use both doors to keep traffic moving. Just make sure people enter from the back and walk to their chair from behind the audience.

MICROPHONE

Is this thing on? If you've got a decent-sized number of attendees, then you need a microphone. If you have a smaller setting, you don't have to worry about this, but the volume of the speaker is a vital part of the meeting. If you have 125-plus people in a room, there will be noise and you need a microphone. People will cough, clear their throat, juggle notepads, pens, etc. Check the microphone before the meeting to make sure it works and it sounds clear. Have extra batteries on hand should they be needed. Get your audio levels set where you want them. Check this twice, just in case—before the meeting starts.

WHITEBOARD

People are going to take notes at your meeting. They can't possibly write as fast as you talk. If you have a whiteboard to write on, this will help the audience and you. Write short lists so they can get the pertinent information down in a timely fashion. The other great thing about the whiteboard is that it will help the speaker keep track of what they've covered and the direction they are headed. Please make sure the whiteboard is stabilized and won't roll or fall over if touched. Don't embarrass your speaker by not doing this. Nobody wants to be making a point and knock over a big whiteboard. Have plenty of fresh markers to write with. Bring five if you need two. Bring 20 if you need five. You can't really have too many.

Use the right colors that can be seen easily on the board. Black, Blue, Green and Red are pretty standard colors to use. Don't use yellow or pink because it's not going to show up well. Think about those in the back of the room that want to see what you are writing.

You also need an eraser. Bring four! Check the eraser on the board before the meeting, and make sure it easily cleans off the ink.

Make sure you start the meeting with a clean board, unless you have a theme or phrase you want on the board to open the meeting. If you do have something that needs to be written on the board, make sure it's done well and looks good. If you have terrible penmanship, let somebody else write what you need!

STRAIGHTEN UP THE ROOM

A clean room sets the tone, so make sure you have a clean room that is free of clutter. It should be a professional setting, so make sure it is. Pick up anything left over from a prior meeting, and make sure the chairs are set-up correctly, as discussed earlier. A clean room makes a good first impression and will not detract from the NAA image.

WATER

If your meeting is in a hotel meeting room, the hotel should provide a water station at the rear of the room. Make sure the hotel staff sets it up on time, and has enough glasses and napkins. Have someone on your team keep an eye on the area and keep the table in order. NOTE: Make sure the speaker has what he/she wants to drink. Do this as a courtesy to the speaker so he/she will not have to worry about it.

WALKWAY

Is there space to move comfortably? There should be. Set the room up with a walkway for your audience to get seated, and for your speaker to get to the front of the room easily.

LOBBY

Where's the meeting? If you are in a large hotel, guests may not be able to find the meeting room on their own. Don't rely just on signs. Make sure that you have an agent in the lobby to greet guests and help direct them to the meeting room. Have two agents if you are expecting a large crowd. Having greeters in the lobby will make a very good first impression, especially on first-time visitors. Existing agents should not be conducting a "lobby seminar." They should be in the meeting room.

SIGN IN TABLE

Make sure you have someone at a sign-in table at the door of your meeting room to answer any questions and to assist the guests. It's important that the agent assigned to this duty be outgoing and friendly, because, again, this is an opportunity to make a positive impression on potential new agents. The reputation of NAA is at stake!

OUR GUESTS

Get them to the front! Our guests should be seated in the front row, if possible, because from that spot they have a better chance to catch the excitement and enthusiasm from the speaker. Being close will also make sure they have no distractions and allow them to get good notes. Veteran agents should always sit in the back, since they already know the information being presented.

EMPTY SEATS

The place looks empty? It shouldn't. You never want empty seats. When you set up the room don't put out all the chairs. You always want to have to pull more chairs in as needed. You should always keep a stack of chairs in the back of the room to fill in after all seats are taken. It's always better to have to bring in more chairs than it is to have a bunch of empty seats.

MISTAKES TO AVOID AT A MEETING

BE EARLY, NOT LATE!

Basketball players at the University of North Carolina at Chapel Hill often talk about Dean E. Smith time. Smith, the legendary Tar Heels coach who won two NCAA titles before retiring after 1997-98 season, was famous for always saying, "if you are on time, then you are five minutes late." What did Smith mean by that? He knew that part of being prepared for games, practices, meetings, class, etc…was being early, instead of on time.

To this day, Phil Ford, an All-American point guard at UNC, sets his wristwatch and cell phone 15 minutes fast so that he is never "on time." He calls it being on DES (Dean E. Smith) time. This is a guy who hasn't played for his old coach since the late 1970s, and he has not forgotten that one simple lesson.

Being early sets a positive tone for the people you meet with. Show them how valuable or important you think the meeting is by showing up early. Arriving late shows just the opposite. For most meetings, it's great to be there 30 minutes early. You might be able to help with last-minute details that are needed before your guests arrive, and association with other agents and their guests is invaluable.

DRESS FOR SUCCESS

This should be obvious, but we always have some agents who need to be reminded about proper attire. For opportunity meetings, all our agents should be in business attire, looking professional 100 percent of the time. No exceptions. No shorts, flip flops, T-shirts, etc… Every agent's attire reflects on

> *"Skirts are like paragraphs. They have to be long enough to cover the material, but short enough to keep people interested."*
>
> –Jane Albright

NAA and on every agent's business. For our ladies, dresses, skirts, or business suits are the order of the day, and, of course, making sure your attire is not too revealing.

You know what is appropriate, so be professional. Make sure that guests are informed, too, before they show up. If they don't know what to wear, and they show up "under dressed" we have set them up for embarrassment, and NAA already has one strike against us.

If a current agent comes to any of our business events dressed inappropriately we have to "coach them up" on how to dress. Once you represent NAA, you need to make sure you dress correctly and act professionally.

Your agency manager will cover with you what the proper attire is for going on appointments, attending meetings, and other functions related to NAA. Just keep in mind that you're in business for yourself, but you represent NAA and our carriers, and we do business in public.

LEAVE PROBLEMS AT THE DOOR

If you've had a bad day, argued with a friend or relative, or are in a bad mood, please don't bring that into the meeting. Your attitude will impact others. We all know life can have its moments, but this is a people business. People don't want to hear about your personal problems, traffic jams, or even bad weather. LEAVE IT AT THE DOOR.

DO NOT WAIT FOR GUESTS IN THE PARKING LOT

Don't wait in the parking lot or even the lobby for people, because then you look desperate to get people in the meeting. If guests can find the parking lot, then they can find the meeting. An agent will be in the lobby to greet guests and can point them in the right direction, so you don't need to linger in the parking lot!

ARE YOU IN, OR ARE YOU OUR?

When you go to a meeting, stay in the meeting. This is part of your "job" so treat it that way. You are there to learn from others, and you are there to help people that have questions for you. You are there to work the system and build your business. Do not hide in an office, spend pointless time on your laptop, or cell phone and then walk into the room when the meeting is over.

Your team might see this and duplicate it in the future. Other teams might think you are doing what you are supposed to be doing, when, in fact, you are doing just the opposite. You could hurt your business, and you could hurt other people's business. Be there in the meeting, or do not go at all. Support the team.

BE EXCITED

Every time one of the speakers finishes, you need to be excited even if you have heard them speak 1,000 times. Don't act casually about them being at your meeting. Treat all speakers like you have never heard them before. Don't forget where you came from. Do you remember the first time you saw the presentation? Wasn't it powerful? Be excited this time too! Guests are watching how NAA agents act, and EVERY agent has a responsibility to the team.

WHAT TO SAY AFTER THE MEETING

When the meeting is over and you meet with guests, what you say to them is just as important as the presentation. Instead of asking them what they think, you want to say something positive and affirmative. Here are just a couple examples:

- Wasn't that a great presentation?

- This is a great opportunity, isn't it?

- The speaker is very good, wouldn't you say?

- Now you see why I asked you to attend this meeting?

ANSWERING TOO MANY QUESTIONS BEFORE SETTING UP AN INTERVIEW

You are going to have guests that are very excited and curious to know more about the opportunity and the business. If they are really excited, they're going to want to ask questions, a lot of questions. Don't make the mistake of doing your upline's job too early! Instead of answering their questions, tell them it is great that they have questions. Tell them they have great questions and you are happy they're interested. Ask them to write their questions down so when they come back the next day to meet with you and your manager, they are prepared. You can say, "When you come back to meet with "John Smith" tomorrow, he will answer all your questions!"

Don't talk too much! When you are new, you might not know how to properly answer the questions. Remember, if it's not your meeting, you need to yield to your upline. Learn from the experts. Before long, you'll be the expert that new agents defer to with their guests.

PROPER ROOM SETUP DIAGRAM

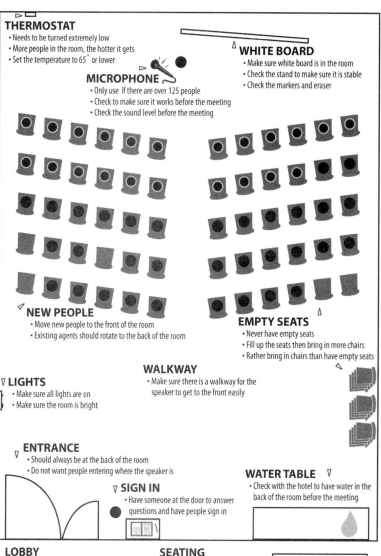

THERMOSTAT
- Needs to be turned extremely low
- More people in the room, the hotter it gets
- Set the temperature to 65° or lower

MICROPHONE
- Only use if there are over 125 people
- Check to make sure it works before the meeting
- Check the sound level before the meeting

WHITE BOARD
- Make sure white board is in the room
- Check the stand to make sure it is stable
- Check the markers and eraser

NEW PEOPLE
- Move new people to the front of the room
- Existing agents should rotate to the back of the room

EMPTY SEATS
- Never have empty seats
- Fill up the seats then bring in more chairs
- Rather bring in chairs than have empty seats

WALKWAY
- Make sure there is a walkway for the speaker to get to the front easily

LIGHTS
- Make sure all lights are on
- Make sure the room is bright

ENTRANCE
- Should always be at the back of the room
- Do not want people entering where the speaker is

SIGN IN
- Have someone at the door to answer questions and have people sign in

WATER TABLE
- Check with the hotel to have water in the back of the room before the meeting

LOBBY
- Have someone at the front lobby to greet people and direct them to the room

SEATING
- Set up theatre style
- No desk or tables at the seats

STRAIGHTEN UP
- Pick up all the trash and stuff lying around
- Make the room look professional

● People
◐ New People
▮ Chairs

NAA HOT SPOT CHECK LIST

☐ **THERMOSTAT**
- More people in the room the hotter it gets
- Set the temperature to 65 degrees or lower

☐ **LIGHTS**
- Make sure the room is bright

☐ **CHAIRS**
- Set up theatre style—minimal number, and be prepared to add more
- No desk or tables at the seats
- Never have empty seats; you can always add chairs later
- Fill up the seats then bring in more chairs

☐ **ENTRANCE**
- Entrance should always be at the back of the room
- Do not want people entering the front where the speaker is

☐ **MICROPHONE**
- Only use the microphone if there is over 125 people
- Check to make sure it works properly and sound level is tested before the meeting

☐ **STRAIGHTEN UP THE ROOM**
- Make the room look professional
- Pick up all the trash and stuff lying around

☐ **WHITEBOARD**

- Make sure whiteboard is in the room and clean
- Check the stand to make sure it is stable
- Check the markers on the whiteboard
- Check the eraser on the whiteboard

☐ **WATER**

- Check with the hotel to have water in the back of the room before the meeting

☐ **WALKWAY**

- Make sure there is a walkway for the speaker to enter the room and get to the front easily

☐ **LOBBY**

- Have someone at the front of the lobby to greet people and direct them to the room

☐ **SIGN IN**

- Have someone who is friendly and smiles at the door to answer questions and have people sign in to the meeting

☐ **GUESTS**

- Move New people to the front of the room
- Existing agents should rotate to the back of the room and sit
- Do not stand along the back wall and talk throughout the meeting

BOOK A MEETING FROM A MEETING

BAMFAM is an acronym that simply means Book A Meeting From A Meeting. As you contact each person on your list and you get a "depends," "yes," or "I need to find out more," then you need to book a meeting from that telephone call. It's critical that you have a date, a specific time, and a specific place to meet from there. Every time you meet with someone, book the next SPECIFIC meeting.

At the end of our business briefing you need to have an organized wrap-up with your guest.

WHAT'S THE WRAP-UP LOOK LIKE?

Let's say you've done everything perfectly. You called the person, did a qualifying interview, they confirmed they were coming to meeting, and they came. You sat them in the front row. You edified the speaker with the guest prior to the meeting. The speaker was great. The meeting was great.

Toward the end of the meeting, the speaker will bring up other leaders in the room, to give a short, two-minute personal testimony. Doing this transfers credibility from the speaker to the other leaders. It's quick, and whatever they say, you respond positively. You ask the guest what they liked best about the presentation and then introduce him/her to the speaker, other leaders, and other agents you feel they can easily relate to.

If you are the host of a new prospect you have three big objectives:

- Introduce new people to the main speaker or other leaders at the meeting; Edify the speaker to build up their credibility and the speaker will, in turn, edify you.

- Give the new person materials, books, carrier literature, multiple CDs, The 8 Steps to Success,
- BAM-FAM (within 48 hours)

Before you introduce the guest to one of our leaders, if possible, give the leader as much information about the guest as you can, so they can know what direction to take the conversation. The leader will then edify the agent to the guest. He's basically going to tee it up for you and let you set up the next meeting. After visiting with the guest for a while, that leader who built you up, is going to move out of the picture and you are going to take over. Your job now is to load up the guest with material to take with them. You then need to set up another meeting for the next 24 to 48 hours right then. You have to BAM-FAM them. Book A Meeting From A Meeting RIGHT NOW.

It's OK to do a follow-up at 5:30 a.m. or 11:30 p.m.; it's OK to drive five hours to meet with somebody. Just don't let too much time go by so that they don't remember what they were excited about at the meeting. You have to follow-up and get them moving forward and moving fast! In 48 hours, people are going to forget details and the emotion that had them excited. The emotion is what moves them forward to the next step to get a license, start ExamFX, get contracted, create a warm-market list, etc…So your next step…BAMFAM!

Time and place doesn't matter. It can be lunch. It can be a telephone call. However, doing it in person is ideal. It doesn't matter; just make it happen. Book that meeting. Do it in 24 to 48 hours…ALWAYS!

If you have to send a guest to a meeting that you cannot attend let your guests know you will not be at the meeting and put them in touch with a leader who will be at the meeting and can be their host. This leader will do all the things you would do—introduce the guest to the speaker and let the speaker know who sent them.

The speaker will edify you and encourage the guest to call you A.S.A.P. after the meeting and you can take the next step—BAMFAM.

Our agents should treat all our managers and speakers as a big deal. Their time is important, so it is a big deal that they are in attendance. They are incredible producers and team members and need to be held in the highest regard. We want to edify our speakers no matter what you really think of them. It's not about you, it's about the team. Doing this helps with setting up the next meeting when the speaker puts the credibility back on you.

Remember to use BAM-FAM right after the meeting. Don't leave it hanging in the balance. You can't say you booked a meeting just because you told a guest you'd call them sometime tomorrow. That is not specific enough. It has to be more exact than that. It needs to be an exact time. It can be just a phone call, but it must be scheduled at a specific time.

It drives me crazy when a company like Time Warner Cable wants to schedule its appointments in windows of four hours, where you —the customer—have to basically be tied to your home until the cable guy finds time in his busy schedule to service your house. To me, that's not a good model. That might be part of the reason I have DirecTV too.

How can you ask somebody that is paying you for a monthly service to choose a block of four hours? That is not specific enough for me. If I'm offering something to a client, then I want to set an exact time. How about 9:05 a.m.? Does that work for you? If they say yes, there is no confusion. We are going to meet at 9:05 a.m. SHARP! Not how about from noon to 4 p.m.? Can you spare four hours of your life for me to plug a cable into a box? No way!

What if something comes up in that window and my cable guy hasn't come yet? Can I leave and get back before he arrives? I don't know, so I'm stuck in limbo while he's out doing no telling what somewhere else. That's just not good enough for me. That's why we use BAMFAM.

Respect other people's time like it's your own. Be on time, be specific, and don't leave things open-ended when trying to follow up with people. Be firm and have them commit to a specific follow up time.

If it is within a couple of hours after the presentation, you should meet with this guest face-to-face at a restaurant, hotel lobby, or your office. I always book a specific meeting place and time to get back with an important person. In the beginning stages of a relationship, it's important that you make contact with the person every 24 to 48 hours to build that strong business relationship.

You do not want more than 48 hours to pass without you getting in front of this prospect eyeball to eyeball, kneecap to kneecap. That's the way relationships are built. That's the way business is conducted. This essentially will not be a challenge if the prospect is really excited and ready to move forward.

In addition to using BAMFAM, it's good to give the prospect something to do—homework if you want to call it that—before your next meeting. It might be to read something, or it might be to go look at a Web site. One great tool would be to give them the NAA newsletter or one of our MP3s. Give them too much to do! People will be more excited that you think they're capable of doing those tasks than if you don't give them anything to do. By giving them an assignment or assignments, you will quickly find out if a prospect really is someone you want as a business partner.

If there is a big meeting, such as a Fall Forward event, National Convention, or a Leadership Conference coming up, you should get it on the recruit's calendar and then turn around and book the meeting, within 24 to 48 hours, of course. This continuity of meetings will enhance your relationship, therefore building your network of clients and business associates.

It's that simple. Always BAMFAM. Watch you business grow! Watch your bank account grow!

10 Great Tips to Help BAMFAM

- Set an exact time to meet the person in the next 24 to 48 hours

- Give the person an assignment to complete before your next meeting

- Write down the time of your next meeting in a NAActivity book you told them about

- Meet face to face (if possible)

- Load them up with materials about products, carriers and NAA

- Prepare questions for them

- Be prepared to answer their questions

- Tell them about the next, big upcoming event and get it on their calendar

- Exchange e-mail, phone numbers

- Repeat BAMFAM! Book the next meeting!

ANDY ALBRIGHT'S 8 STEPS TO SUCCESS

1. Personal Use
2. Work
3. Listen
4. Read
5. Attend ALL Meetings
6. Be Teachable
7. Be Accountable
8. Communicate with a positive mental attitude

A NOTE ABOUT THE 8 STEPS

When I wrote my first book, *The 8 Steps to Success*, it was a blueprint for people to change what they were doing and to enjoy a better life personally and professionally.

Part of our system involves following the 8 Steps. I'm going to cover a little of each step in the following chapter, just to give you an idea of what it takes to implement each step. You still need to get a copy of *The 8 Steps to Success*, but here is a small taste of what that book contains.

People come up to me all the time and tell me how my simple steps have changed their outlook on life. They share with me how their family is happier now than ever before because they've reached a better place in life.

I want this manual or blueprint of what our successful people do, along with the 8 Steps, to make your life better too. Write down how many of the steps you are already following and take note of the ones you need to work on. Make a list of things you can do better and start to work on those.

If you dedicate yourself to following the 8 Steps then you will start to see a difference in your life. It will not happen overnight, but, with continued, consistent effort, it will help you.

Pay close attention to the next few pages and focus on how you can implement the 8 Steps in your life and business.

The eight steps were written to be very simple, but when you start to peel back all the layers and get deeper, it might seem hard to do all eight things all the time. They're not really that difficult, but if you follow them all—100%—then it seems like a lot. It's not impossible, but you have to commit to doing it all the time. Do it consistently and you'll start seeing success in your NAA business.

STEP 1: THE IMPORTANCE OF PERSONAL USE

If you were a business owner, let's say you own Coke or Pepsi, then you should probably drink your own product.

If you don't believe in what you sell and use it yourself, then why should others purchase your product from you?

I tell people all the time that personal use can be as important in helping grow your sales and your business as anything you do.

The first thing you should do is invest in your product before you even think about trying to go out and make a sale. Forget the commission that is out there. If you don't have your own policy, that's like a football player telling his coach he wants to play a few games before he decides whether or not he wants to bother learning the playbook! You can't have a guy on your team like that.

If you own what you offer then you have a higher credibility and believability factor than a company or person that doesn't use or own the service they provide.

Beyond that, you are more likely to be comfortable asking others to buy or own your products if you can tell them face-to-face or over the phone that, "hey, it's good enough for me and I think you need it too!"

After you own your product, practice your selling technique by seeing if your family or friends also need the products you offer. This helps you work on dealing with people, and you are also doing what you think is right by the people you care about.

Again, you are building credibility with people. Your belief in the products you offer will also grow by doing this.

Integrity establishes a baseline and a firm foundation for everything you do. As a business owner, agent, etc., integrity begins with knowing, believing and investing in the products or services you offer. How can you represent something you don't own yourself?

Being part of an organization requires participation, and that means buying in—literally—to the business and its services.

Beyond owning something you offer, you also should know the product you are selling. Why?

You can only be effective at selling the product if you know the product, believe in it, and can explain why it's needed to a potential client.

Selling requires making a commitment. The very act of studying a product, learning enough about it to convince yourself that the product is a good one, should lead to you selling yourself on the product and then selling the product to others.

Ask yourself this: would you purchase an annuity or life insurance policy from an agent who did not own a policy himself? Would you trust this agent? Would you trust the very company he works for?

If you own what you sell, life will be much easier for you when it comes to selling!

Your clients don't care what the commission is for you on a product, but they do care about what the product will offer them, should they choose to purchase a policy from you.

The more you know about products, the more credibility you will gain with people. Over time, people with tell their friends and family how you helped them and made sure they were covered with the right product, and it will help grow your list of clients and book of business.

Growing up, I heard of people getting fired from Coke because they were caught drinking Pepsi! Smart employees probably drank the competition when others were not around, but there was a huge risk in doing that. I like that rule. If you don't like what you sell, you shouldn't work for that company.

Being loyal to your brand indicates your belief in the product. You should own and purchase it no matter what it is, be it soft drinks, cars, vitamins, juice, or life insurance!

You should be a walking advertisement for the company and product you offer.

Knowing, believing, and investing in your product are all important because all sales begin with emotion. People make up their minds based on feelings, then back their decisions with logic. If you understand emotionally what it's like to purchase your product, then you will see the logic in owning a life insurance policy to protect your family.

Knowing, believing, and investing in your own product will establish a baseline of integrity you need to get going in the field!

Make the first commitment to yourself. After that, you can focus on helping the client. If you can convince yourself, you should be able to convince others to own the products you are selling.

You must make your business personal, and you must do it now by starting with personal use.

STEP 2: ARE YOU WILLING TO DO THE WORK?

Work requires effort, no matter the occupation. Work also requires staying focused, and it requires staying motivated to attain your goals.

When you look through magazines and see lavish homes, dream vacation spots and fancy cars, do you think about how you are going to work to have those things, or do you say something like, "It must be nice to be rich." When you have the desire to donate money to charities or other needed causes, do you wish you could help?

Motivation comes from wants and desires. Like the Gatorade ad says, "Is it in you?"

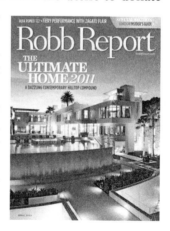

People that lack that motivation are the people that are just happy and content with what they have, and they don't strive for anything more.

What an individual wants typically dictates his drive and motivation.

The *Robb Report* is a great publication if you want to see global luxury items.

People that are able to overcome deficiencies and obstacles are motivated. They fight through whatever stands between them and their goals.

Robb Report is a great publication for people to draw out things they dream of owning and doing in the future.

How do they do this?

It starts with action. You gotta move! Even if it is just writing out what you are going to do, that's a start. It's great to have a plan, but once you take the first step then things can change for you.

How fast do you want something?

Can you get that new car now? In five years?

Maybe your goal is to get out of debt, or as I call it, "back to broke!" Can you do that this year?

Setting weekly goals rather than yearly goals will allow you to hit your mark faster than trying to plan 12 months out.

"It won't work unless you work" is another favorite phrase of mine. Beyond that, you also need to learn to work smarter! Set up a work routine and be committed to it. Set dates and then get after it. Most people want to succeed, but they don't follow through. They don't have that fire in their belly that separates average people from great people in business.

Are you afraid of work? If you are, you probably aren't totally happy with your life and your career.

Enjoy working? Great. Now, make sure your work is effective work that is pushing you closer to your goals.

What do you want? What is it that you are willing to really work for?

Most people are not motivated by luxury items to start with— most just want to pay the bills and have some left over at the end of the month.

A lot of people work hard, but seemingly get little done. Others seem like they don't work that hard, but they always seem to come out on top. The latter is probably an effective worker that is goal-oriented and focused on results!

Make a list of objectives and chase them like your life depends on it. Unleash your calculated attack on your goals and, over time, you will find what it means to truly be free financially and you will enjoy what you do professionally on a daily basis.

One effective way to reach your goals is by working in bursts of concentrated effort for long amounts of time. You might work 60 hours a week and only be away from home for three days. To do this, however, you need to be very organized and that will allow you to enjoy more free time with family and friends.

Another important factor in success is finding what you love and figuring out how to do that!

USE THESE FOUR WAYS TO WORK MORE EFFECTIVELY AND SEE WHAT RESULTS YOU PRODUCE:

- Make a list of things you need/want to do
- Prioritize your list and attack each task
- Do one thing on the list that you don't want to do
- Keep records of your progress (Do this daily, and at the end of the week to see where you stand.)

Work requires making the right commitment, following the program you've put in place, and adapting it to your plan of attack. Be methodical and track your activity. This means monitoring your checklist so you—YOU—can measure your performance.

Think of it like you are a doctor in business. A doctor uses vital signs to decide what direction of action is needed. Your vitals can be your checklist. It should reveal strengths and weaknesses for you to work on. Your records are proof that you have worked. You can almost predict what is going to happen with your business based on your records.

If you feel like you are working effectively and you are not seeing desired results, then PLEASE CHANGE SOMETHING!

Focus on the following things: attitude, work ethic, character. Those are three things that you can control. Work to improve in those three areas.

Don't be afraid to fail. At least you are trying and showing that you are motivated. Take action because you will never hit something if you don't take dead aim. The more times you shoot for something the better the chances that you will hit it!

Sitting around will lead to failure and it can be contagious. Don't wait for success to find you because it will not. Work, work, and work will lead you to success's doorstep.

Excitement, conviction, and execution are the name of the game.

By putting forth concentrated effort, you will see results!

STEP 3: HAVE YOU LEARNED TO LISTEN?

Do you have different levels of listening? You probably do and do not want to admit it.

How many times have you nodded or said "uh huh" to a person and you really didn't process a word they just said to you?

This can't happen when you are conducting business.

Many ideas are communicated only when the listener pays attention to more than just the words that are spoken. Great communication is achieved only when people use their EYES, EARS and their MINDS! It takes all three to become a great active listener.

Most successful people are active listeners. They listen to what their partners are telling them, they listen to what clients are saying, and they pay attention to what other successful people are doing. They are successful because they stay actively involved. They absorb information both through the words they hear and the speaker's body language.

Listen to Learn

Active listening is an important key to knowing your customer, and good listening skills usually have to be cultivated. Even sharp people often have poor listening skills by nature. Being a good listener is a rare ability, but with practice can be learned by anybody.

Our society is filled with audible distractions and devices that would easily prevent a person from really listening. Because of that, being able to block all that out and focus on what is being said is even more important.

"Listen" is a verb. It indicates action and activity. What action is involved in listening? There's no action! Really? So, your ears just work automatically? Listening requires mental and physical activity from YOU!

Imagine you talking to a person. Are you taking notes? If you are, you are hearing and seeing at the same time.

Are you looking at the person? You should be. You can listen with your eyes too. You can see the person's body language. That is meaningful information you are collecting just by watching

Being a great listener really means being a good communicator, because when you listen you should be translating the words so you know the intended meaning of what you are hearing. You have to be engaged in the conversation to know what you are really being told.

If a potential client is talking to you, is the look on his/her face in agreement with his words, or does his facial expression tell a different story? Be sure you know, or you might miss the truth. If you miss the truth, you just might miss the sale!

Listen to Understand

There are five great ways to help you understand people better. If you follow these steps, you will be a better listener. You will also stop worrying about making a sale when you are in somebody's house. You will help the potential client be more comfortable too. It takes time and practice to master the craft of listening, but these five rules will help you improve your ability to listen.

- Don't interrupt: Allow the speaker to convey his thoughts without rushing to convey your thoughts and ideas. This shows respect and genuine interest.

- Sit down: If the situation presents itself, sit directly in front of the speaker. This lets the speaker know he has your full attention and that you are committed to what he has to say.

- Maintain eye contact: Face the speaker. Keep your mind open to receive the information. Maintain eye contact and occasionally nod your head to let the speaker know you comprehend what he is saying. If you are in a meeting or conference, it might be impossible to maintain eye contact. In these situations, it is OK to take notes to reinforce key information, and to show you are paying attention.

- Acknowledge his words: An occasional head nod shows the speaker you are actively engaged in what he is saying. Audible affirmations such as "yes," "by all means," "that is true" or "I understand" are completely acceptable.

- End with open questions: When the speaker has finished his thoughts, end the discussion with a couple of open questions. These questions should require more than just a "yes" or "no" answer.

Another thing that is effective in listening is to mimic people mentally or duplicate the facial expressions of the person speaking. Treat the speaker like a performer in a play that you need to be able to duplicate. Can you repeat what the person has said? Can you mimic their expressions? This helps to understand what the person wants me to know.

Recording conversations—when appropriate—is another great way to improve your listening skills. It also makes you an active listener because you had to think to bring a recorder before you even arrived at your meeting, seminar, etc.

Listening While Selling

When you are in a client's home and you are trying to make a sale, you can mimic your clients. I don't mean sit in front of them and make the exact same face they do. They will think you are making fun of them. I mean position your body the way they are sitting in order to feel what they are feeling.

You can pick up on things the person is thinking without them even saying it. You will understand them better.

Listen without any preconceived notions of what the other person will say. You should not enter conversations—especially when trying to make a sale—with a bunch of preconceived notions in your mind. Don't assume anything! Just listen to the person and be genuinely interested in what is being communicated.

MAKE YOUR CAR A ROLLING UNIVERSITY

Many people spend hours of time in their cars on a daily basis. Do they use that time to be productive? Some do. Others spend that time listening to sports radio, talk radio, or the latest single from Lady Gaga.

Instead of doing that, what people should do is make phone calls—safely—and listen to audio that will help them grow their business, improve their skills, and help them live a better life.

Motivated business people use their time wisely and sharpen their minds even when they are just riding in the car. It makes the time go by faster too.

Active listening should be diligently practiced. This habit will help advance your career by sending a message to your clients that you have a sincere interest in them and not just making a sale. It tells management that you are eager to learn and want to excel in your business.

STEP 4: ARE YOU READING?

Whether you read one chapter a day or one page a day, you must read. It's not optional for successful people. It's a must.

There is too much information at your fingertips not to continue learning. Even if you are at the top of your occupation, you still don't know everything.

An old wise man once said that "all the secrets of the universe were once kept in libraries that only an elite few could access. With access to these secrets, the elite few dominated the world."

Today, books are where you are. On shelves, on iPads, Kindles, iPhones, BlackBerry, etc…You have no reason not to read something daily. Trade publications, newspapers, books…just read!

Anybody can access them. However, the wise man is right. Those who take advantage of that "access" by reading will succeed over those who do not. The choice is yours. Choose to read!

When you open a book, you should learn something new. If you are having trouble getting started, try tearing out a single page and taking it with you during your day. When you have a break during your day, pull it out and read it.

It is illegal to tear up money, but there is nothing illegal about tearing up a book that you own. At first, it will feel odd because we are not accustomed to tearing up books. As children, we are taught not to tear up or mark in books. Put away those childish ways.

Also, if you are not accustomed to reading, it will feel odd for your brain to receive information from a source other than the television or radio. Even if it is just for 15 to 20 minutes a day, you should be reading! You have to read! Whatever it takes, start reading.

If you read a book or an article that you find useful, don't forget it. Over time, it's fine to read things over and over again. If it puts you back in the right mindset, that's what you should do.

If you read something a second time and want to highlight parts of the book, use a different color highlighter so you can see what stood out each time you read the chapter, book, article, etc.

Successful people usually are avid readers. They read everything from books to billboards and advertisements. They also read information they can find on their competition! Reading puts you ahead of the curve. Allow books to become your mentors, help your business, increase your knowledge, and then use that knowledge to improve your position in business.

If I could suggest one book to read outside of my *The 8 Steps to Success*, it would be *Read and Grow Rich* by Burke Hedges. It talks all about the importance of reading. I encourage you to get it and start reading it today!

Read to Sell

If I want people in my organization to be successful in business, I "trick" them into reading. Yes, I am willing to trick people into becoming smarter and more successful!

If I see somebody consistently making the same mistakes, I can handle it in one of two ways. I can tell them directly and forcibly, possibly jeopardizing the relationship, or I can point to a book that will convey the same message in a way more likely to be accepted and appreciated. That is my trick.

The book is dispassionate, but it can light a fire under them and cause them to change for the better. I like to get people fired up, and one way to do that is to get people to read success stories and motivational books.

A book's ideas or message can change your thought patterns and your success in business and life. I have seen people read just the right book they needed and it sets them on fire. They are enthusiastic and energized, which yields higher production.

Reading gets your brain moving rapidly, page after page, and helps you build momentum. Books can change your mindset and that can make all the difference in the world for you professionally and personally.

I have a suggested reading list of books that I have read time and time again. You can check it out at www.andyalbright.com/booklist.

I hope you will review my list and start reading!

STEP 5: WHY YOU MUST ATTEND ALL MEETINGS

Ask any successful person and they will tell you how important it is to attend meetings. People don't schedule and hold meetings for their health. There is a reason for having meetings, and you should attend them all as if they were mandatory.

I don't care if it is a sales meeting, a seminar or a weekend convention, if the people who run my organization are going, then I'm going. I'm there—no question.

It's those types of meetings where the best training can be found where you learn how to do simple, little things that can make all the difference in your business. You also get to meet with other members of your team, network, and learn from others.

When a person attends a meeting, he is sending a clear message that he wants to be part of the organization. This person also sees value in the company's methods and wants to benefit from them.

Attending meetings generates enthusiasm and motivation. It initiates questions. Successful people are excited about attending meetings. They know meetings are a teaching mechanism, designed to keep everyone informed about company products and services. They are a prime venue for networking with other agents and clients.

By creating opportunities for discussion, meetings provide information that will help you track performance, goals, and profitability. They will also help you learn how to sell through associating with other people who are successful.

People get excited when they get outside their comfort zones, and meetings sometimes provide opportunities to get outside that zone. Getting out of that happy, easy place often creates the desire to push to do more, earn more, and grow more professionally.

If the meeting can impact you immediately, why in the world wouldn't you be there? The meetings are designed to give you an edge in what you do. Take advantage of them! You should be willing to fight and scratch for information to make yourself successful.

Now, there is a difference in attending and just showing up. A lot of people sign up and attend events, but don't get any benefit from them. It's the people that are willing to learn, actively listen, take notes, and pay attention that will get ahead.

Do you want to be the person that does just enough to get by, or do you want to be the person chasing real success? The choice is up to YOU!

Meet to Learn

In sales, it is vital that you put your ego aside and try to understand the needs of the person or client you are selling. If a client detects a sense of arrogance on your part, all of the logic and sales techniques in the world will not make him purchase from you. This should carry over to all areas of your business and especially in regards to attending meetings.

Getting around the best leaders in your organization will help you because those people want you to succeed. They can see your desire and they will help you! If you have not obtained a level that enables you to lead sales meetings or to host seminars, then you definitely should be attending them.

There are plenty of ways to change your life. You can READ. You can LISTEN to audio. You can ASSOCIATE with successful people. Do all three, but certainly make sure that you take advantage of any chance you have to meet face to face with top income earners.

Only Losers Complain

People who don't want to attend meetings always have an excuse. The excuse doesn't even have to make sense. They'll use things like finances, family, didn't have a baby sitter, forgot the time, etc…to not attend. They don't see the value of being there and learning. Most of the time, those people are not successful in business.

People who attend all meetings don't complain about doing so. It is the people who refuse to benefit from meetings, who complain about them. Complainers lose because they are not taking advantage of the opportunity, and then they justify in their minds that they didn't miss out on anything.

Grow to Know, Go to Grow

Meetings and conventions allow you to meet face-to-face with people and make direct contact with them. They also allow you to learn from those "who are in the hunt" and have had success beyond what you have tasted. Nothing is more essential to learning than talking to those types of people.

These meetings also generate an excitement level that is hard to create. They open you up to success by getting you excited about making sales. Telephone conversations and e-mail simply do not provide the same value. They lack the personal contact that is important when creating relationships and exchanging ideas.

Direct contact creates the opportunity to form a relationship because it makes it personal. Seeing top performers can teach you new techniques and provide you with better communication skills to help you succeed. Attending meetings allows you the chance to associate with successful people. Their energy and motivation levels are contagious. Get around people with positive attitudes and avoid those who think negatively.

Successful people are driven, motivated, energetic and positive thinkers. They are winners. If you do not associate yourself with winners, how can you expect to win? Take advantage of learning from people by attending all meetings, seminars, and conventions. There is much to be gained in doing this, and so little to lose.

STEP 6: ARE YOU COACHABLE IN YOUR OCCUPATION?

People can change when they want to change. If you change fast, that indicates you want to change. If you change slowly, that indicates you do not want to change. Being "coachable" or teachable means that you want to change and you are willing to do it fast. You are looking for something better.

Finding people in your organization who want to change can make you look like a genius. You have to become a good "finder" of people and a good judge of character. People will give you credit for changing people, and all you did was find people who wanted to change.

For a long time, I was not teachable, and the change was a gradual one for me. I fought change until I was 35. Only then did I really start becoming successful. Had I not fought this, then I would have experienced success faster, instead of thinking I was smarter than everybody else.

How do I do this?

Speed up your growth. Be an accelerator. Time, money and emotion are invested resources. The longer it takes you to change, the more time, money, and emotion you are wasting. Do you want results? Do you want to change your life for the better? If the answer is yes, be willing to make the necessary sacrifices, to change, to invest your time, money and emotions to achieve results. If you are teachable, you can change before your mistakes cause you pain.

People can always become better. They can always do more. A big part of that happening is their willingness to change and re-focus on objectives.

Consider that every time you steer off a correct path by one degree and continue on, you keep compounding the distance between the correct path and where you are going the longer you continue. Over days and weeks, that one degree takes you wider and wider off the path you should be on. In the short run, there is not much of a variation, but over time the difference between "right" and "wrong" will become greatly exaggerated.

With constant correction and guidance, you can correct the course. By watching what you are doing, and by listening to somebody who sees you getting off course, you can always make a correction. You have to be open to what a good mentor can show you, though. You have to be teachable, and willing to change your direction when necessary.

If you are teachable, it means that you are ready, willing, and able to change. You must be ready to accept the challenge and sacrifices change demands. Can you get rid of the useless and harmful habits in your life—habits that do not lend themselves to you being successful?

Now is the best time to make a decision to change your life. The only thing holding you back is you. Develop that winning mindset deep within you. Find your passion, develop the drive and ambition to find success. How do I do this? You have to find the "why," or reason, you want to change your life. Every person's "why" is different, but finding what motivates you is the key.

Always look for means of self-improvement. Sometimes this means taking a step back and gathering your energies. Once you do that, set a game plan, begin with the end in mind, but then work that plan step by step. You can't reach the top in one day.

It is a process. If you have an instruction book telling you how to put something together, then why wouldn't you follow it? If you try to put together a model plane without instructions, it's likely you will be left holding spare pieces.

What keeps people from being teachable?

The biggest impediment to becoming teachable is the influence of other people. Associating with the wrong people can have a terrible impact on you and could be why you are not able to achieve your goals. Being around people that are negative and say things like "can't," "won't" or "aren't" is a bad idea. Those are not the people you need to be around. Find people that want you to be successful and spend time around them.

Take out a sheet of white paper and write down three names of people you need to spend more time around. Now, write down three names of people you need to spend less time around. Doing this will help you focus on finding positive people that want you to succeed in life. Get around those people as much as possible.

Get out of your comfort zone and change! Don't be like I was in my 20s. Don't be so smart that you prevent yourself from being successful. Break the chain. Make it a habit to be positive and speak positively to others. If you have been limited by others in the past, make a decision to break that cycle now. Learn to change and pass that along. Be teachable and then teach others.

STEP 7: ARE YOU ACCOUNTABLE?

What does it mean to be accountable? It means you do what you say you are going to do.

It means you are who you say you are. This sounds easy, but it would shock you just how many people can't follow this simple step. Do you follow this? Ask a trusted friend to tell you how well you are at following through on your promises. Do your actions reflect what you say to other people?

It's important to be accountable for your actions, be it good or bad. When you do this, you become more committed to your goals. Being accountable requires being committed in all areas of your life. Not only must you work, you must also prepare FOR work.

Professional athletes dream from an early age of making it to the top. That dream doesn't just happen for them. They work for it. They train and exercise. They sacrifice crazy amounts of time, just to have a shot at the pros.

If you expect to be a leader in business, you have to have those same solid work habits. If you aren't working hard, how can you expect others to do so? This goes for clients and co-workers. If you don't follow through, people will lose confidence and trust in you. This loss of confidence, trust, and accountability often leads to a loss of sales.

In the next 90 days, can you make a commitment to change your attitude and to hold yourself accountable for your actions and words?

If you can do this, you will find yourself in a position of strength, instead of a position of weakness. Your biggest enemy is your own mind. If you spend time thinking negatively, you will never find time to think positively. Commit and change. Be responsible for your actions. Rather than taking two steps forward and three steps back, reverse the downward spiral and make your life one of constant forward movement.

Do not lie to yourself. Set goals, but make sure your goals are logical and attainable. Don't set impossible or unlikely goals for yourself that will force you to back off when you see those goals aren't possible. Let your goals be like promises you make to yourself, and only make promises that you know you can keep (Be accountable to yourself).

Being able to keep promises you make is vital in business. It sounds great to a client when you promise them the moon and the stars, but when you fail to deliver you'll have a big problem. Clients trust you. If you say you will deliver, then you better be able to. Don't say things you really don't mean. Don't promise what you aren't sure you can deliver. It hurts your self-confidence, because not only does the client see your lack of accountability, you see it too!

Start with small goals that will develop your character before you start talking about huge goals or long-term goals. When you can deliver on small promises, you will start to see you can deliver more. Develop slowly by tackling goals you know you can handle. Find out what you can handle and raise the bar over time. Being accountable on small scales will lead to handling bigger things.

Make yourself accountable for your life. Commit yourself to find the positive and eliminate the negative in your life. Your outlook WILL determine your outcome!

STEP 8: THE POWER OF COMMUNICATING WITH A POSITIVE ATTITUDE

Your ability to communicate conveys a message about your personality. Are you constantly finding reasons to complain? Are you finding fault in your co-workers and friends? Communication can be destructive or constructive.

You have to make a conscious decision that you are not going to complain. Ask more questions instead of always making comments or statements. Asking questions tells others that you are anxious to learn and that you are interested in what they have to say. Positive communication indicates your desire to be of service. Communicating in a positive manner will lure people into your business.

Projecting a positive mental attitude is something that can be learned, just like anything else. If you wake up in the morning, you should be excited. You just woke up in the United States and you are free to work as little or as much as you want! That's being positive about life.

Get excited about being alive, drop the negative mindset and focus on the positive! You will encounter negatives at some point, but if you've built a positive mindset you can handle adversity in a much better way.

How you say it matters.

Choosing the right means of communicating is important. If your message is factual, then communicate with an e-mail or a text message. Telephone numbers, sales figures, and contacts are facts. If your message involves emotions, communicate with a phone call or in person. Use the most effective means of communication for the type of message you have to relay.

It's also important to consider the tone of your communication. It's not all positive, but it can be relayed in a positive tone. Management needs both positive and negative information when it affects business. They need to know when there are problems. They need to be informed of ongoing situations when they occur. However, these things should be conveyed in the most positive context possible.

Communicating your facts and emotions in a positive tone is vital. Words like "we" and "our" rather than "you" or "they" can make the difference in how the message is received. If the team has a problem, it's viewed much differently than a single person feeling like they are being singled out for an issue.

Start with positives. Don't go to your boss or even a co-worker and start harping on negative things right out of the gate. Build up the positives first.

Remember the glass is neither half empty nor half full. It is always full. It is full of water and air. Life is full of failure and negative experiences, but you can start out the day by being happy that you woke up and it's a new day!

It's important to remember that you can't have good or great days without having bad days. Bad days are important. They provide a comparison and allow you to appreciate the good days. It's also important to build on obstacles. They can be the foundation of your success if you build on them instead of letting them destroy you. Make every obstacle or crisis an opportunity to get better.

Maybe you made 100 dials and only set five appointments. Talk about the five you set and not the 95 you missed on. Find the positive and work on improving things from there. It's OK to fail if you learn from it and get better.

Another part of being positive is looking the part. Do you dress for success? Before a word is ever spoken, people are forming an impression and opinion of you based on your appearance. Make sure you are dressed properly for all business situations. If you are ever in doubt of what the dress code is, call your upline and ask them. Doing this conveys an attitude and a confidence in what you are selling. Smile!

How you present yourself will form a lasting impression before you even open your mouth.

When you do open your mouth, make sure your words line up with your thoughts. Keep things positive. If you have questions, you should never be afraid to ask. People will help you learn if you are sincere.

FOUR BASICS
OF RECRUITING

"The only thing holding you back is you. Commit to developing the mindset of a winner, set your goals and chase them down. Remember, a dog in the hunt ain't got no fleas!"

–Andy Albright

THE FOUR BASICS OF RECRUITING

The four "basics" or cornerstones for success in our business for building are the following:

1. The List
2. The Phone Call
3. The Interview
4. The Follow up

When a business of any kind starts, the hardest part is just starting. It's like trying to launch a space shuttle into outer space. I've read that 75 percent of the rocket fuel used during a mission is spent trying to lift the shuttle six inches off the ground. How in the world is that possible?

You are going from a complete standstill to lifting a piece of metal that weighs more than 4.4 million pounds just before takeoff. According to NASA, 1.1 million pounds of that weight is in fuel, but after the shuttle gets six inches off the ground, 75 percent of that fuel has been burned off and the shuttle starts to move faster, climb higher, and the craft begins to cruise toward outer space.

That's not unlike most businesses that are starting up. An entrepreneur spends a lot of energy and effort—the fuel so to speak—in just getting started. That's the hard part.

Once the business is started, then it becomes a matter of repeatedly doing things that work and create success. Success is not about being lucky, it's about being consistent and following the proven basics. This applies to any successful business, sports team, or musical group. CEOs, athletes, and musicians know that practicing the basics and hammering them until things are executed like a well-oiled machine is how you improve and reach the top of your profession. It's no different with National Agents Alliance.

We feel like there are four basic activities that have to be followed and executed in order to be successful. Following the "Four Basics" is highly encouraged at National Agents Alliance if you want to be part of the winning team. If they are not followed, you can't win. If you can't win, how can the team win?

Our "Four Basics" revolve around the following: the list, the phone call, the interview, and the follow up. These are like the cornerstones of a well-built building. They're the strong foundation that supports everything NAA models. When you are working with the NAActivity calendar, you have the four cornerstones on each side of the book. You have the "Four Basics" of recruiting and building your business, and you have the "Four Basics" of selling. It's a 50/50 ratio or model where you have to recruit, and you have to sell. They are equally important. We will focus on the "Four Basics" of recruiting. As we mentioned earlier, you have to work on these four activities when you are recruiting: List, Phone Call, Interview, and Follow Up.

THE LIST

Right out of the gate you start by making a list. It's the first thing you MUST do. Earlier in Chapter 2, we thoroughly covered the importance of compiling a list of prospects. Refer back to this chapter often and keep adding to your list.

When working with a new agent, you should be stressing the importance of creating a list and the hope it can provide for a brighter professional future. This list provides potential future value for your growing business. There's an urgency to make it NOW while you have an upline person who is willing to get with the new agent and work on calling the list right then—in person. Creating the list is an important part of the process and it sets the tone for a person getting started. By establishing a list early, you help set one of the cornerstones of the foundation. The key is to make a list NOW and then ACT on it. MOVE!

The list is the raw material that you mix into the "Four Basics" machine to get things churning and produce the results you desire. Until you start working that list, it cannot yield results. The list is the deal when you start working as a new agent, and you should be able to easily provide 25-50 names immediately. That should be your target; start with at least 25 names. We want you to develop your list and work it, but utilizing your growing upline is the best way to get started. Why wouldn't you take advantage of a person who has worked the business and gotten positive results? It would be foolish not to. Working in your warm-market depth with your upline is going to add credibility to what you are doing because they already know what to say on the initial call. You introduce and edify your upline, you listen and learn from that third-party expert, as you "team up" to call your list. You bring the name, the phone number, and the credibility and reason for the call. This is your warm market. Your upline is your trainer, your teammate. Think of it like a breakaway in basketball. The chances of scoring a basket are much better with you and a teammate working together. A two-on-one gives you an advantage, and most of the time you are going to score an easy layup in this situation.

Before long, you'll be making the calls yourself, and doing calls as the "expert" for your new recruit's list. This duplication process actually begins as soon as the opportunity meeting is over. The posture that you use at that time sets the tone. If your recruit says they like the idea of personal production AND they like the idea of developing an agency, then you should start accessing their list immediately. If you don't work the list in the first 24 hours, then your chances of success will decrease 50 percent each day that you fail to do this. Their belief level will slowly dwindle and fade away. You will miss the chance to build a great relationship and trust with this new agent if you don't move NOW! Get them started when their belief level is as high as it can get. Bottom line: Help them make calls! The faster you get on the list, the better off you will be. Maybe their list has 100 people and you can't call them all that day. That's fine. You can certainly call at least the top five or 10 on the new agent's list. The longer you wait, the harder it will be and the momentum will slow down with your new agent. The longer you sit on that list, the more they will doubt you and they will doubt how much you are willing to help them. Remember, when you're calling this list you are training your new recruit on the process. Follow the system. Do it right and do it right now. Whatever you do, your new recruit will do the exact same thing when they in turn bring on a new agent.

GETTING A LIST

Getting this process started is not rocket science, but there is a methodology to it. Get the recruit writing down names and when the process slows, tell them to pull out their cell phone. There are plenty of names and numbers in their phone!

It might go something like this:

- UPLINE: "Got your cell phone with you? Is there anybody you think would not want to do this in your phone contacts?

- You will get a yes or a no.

- UPLINE: "Who are the top five people you think would want to do this?"

- Have the new agent write the names down.

Keep going. Don't stop until there's a long, long list. The point is to get them thinking and help them start calling the list. If you are the upline, your job is to get that list going. There are two things you want to get a person to do immediately: Get an insurance license (it only takes a week if you try) and generate a list. It is not that hard. It's only two things! Simple!

You can build this business in a mad way or you can do it in a happy way. However, when you build it with passion and emotion you are locked in, focused, and you have a specific goal. If you decide that when you walk out the door every day that you are going to do things with a driven purpose and that you are going to be better today than you were yesterday, then you are going to be successful. If you keep doing that every day, you are going to win most of the time. You'll have some losses, but they will not sting as badly. When you don't win, you'll remember that feeling too. If you desire to be a part of a championship team, you have to work hard. You have to learn how to win. You have to get a little taste of what victory feels like repeatedly until it becomes so etched in your brain that you won't accept defeat. Remembering what it feels like to lose will help you take on that "eye of the tiger" mentality. Put 100 percent effort into the first "Basic"—the List—and emphasize the importance of the list with your new recruits and you've started the strong foundation of a very profitable business.

THE
PHONE CALL

Those little marks you make in the NAActivity book, the number of phone calls you make, are your biggest asset with part two of the "Four Basics." The quantity of calls will yield quality. Yes, the skill level of your call is important, but the more calls you make, the better your success rate will be. You improve by making more calls. You pick up on phrases that work and those that do not. You tweak the direction of your calls based on what you learn from previous calls. Your preference is to get a long list and call in rapid succession. Ready, Fire, Aim. We want you to take action; not wait. We want you to go ahead and shoot before you aim. When you miss, then you can find out why. We will help you, but we want you to get comfortable calling people as fast as possible. You will make mistakes, but you have to keep dialing until you get it right. Make the first call, go through our script, which has variations, and see what the interest level is with each person you call.

The phone call needs to be purposeful and methodical. You are just checking the interest level of a person looking to make outside income. You're not selling NAA or trying to convince the prospect we have the best opportunity on the planet (even though we do!). At this point we're just sorting through your list, gauging interest. It's important you understand the mindset we have—you're the interviewer. You ask the questions and the prospects will quickly qualify themselves as open-minded or not. The posture you take is that we don't hire every person; we're looking for quality people who have something to add to the team. Be confident, keep it simple and remember the basic question: Is this person open to learning more about what we do?

If they are, you want to meet with them in person as fast as possible. How soon? Like right now if they are willing. If they are not close by, use the phone or a webinar, but meeting in person is best. However, you will still use the BAMFAM model. Don't walk away without implementing the BAMFAM method. Once you have found a prospect who is interested in making extra money in addition to their current income, then you need to book another meeting with them…FAST! Try to meet with them several times over the next couple of days. BAMFAM!

THE
INTERVIEW

The purpose of booking the Qualifying Interview ("QI") is to determine if a person is interested in making money through National Agents Alliance. You don't have to be overly aggressive during the interview. Most people confuse the correct posture and control as being hard-nosed or talking to people in an elitist manner. That's not us. The idea is to have a confidence when you talk with a prospect, and help them understand that we have a great model that has worked for us.

BE PREPARED FOR THE INTERVIEW

In the interview, your goal is to ask more questions than the candidate asks you. How do I do that? Be prepared for it. You do want to share information along the way, but you want to get more information from them than you give. For example, let's say you are playing cards. If you have a great hand, you are not going to just announce it to the people playing with you. They will find out soon enough what a good hand you have, just like potential prospects will learn soon enough what National Agents Alliance is building. You can—and should—share informative things like what primary carriers we use, the strategies we employ, the leads system we have, the potential personal income, and our overall group income override strategy. Those are the essentials of our business that will spark the interest of a sharp, business-minded individual that you would want to have on your team.

Again, the main goal is to find out who they are, what they like to do, what their main goals are, and if they fit the profile of what we are looking for. You are not spinning what we do to where the recruit becomes a good fit. You can't force a square peg in a round hole. It's not logical and it won't work, but I've seen people try it.

You should use key phrases like, "we're hiring," "we're looking for a few sharp people," "we use national advertising with CareerBuilder, and we are processing resumes but might make only two or three offers." You can follow up any combination of those statements by saying, "however, we find that sharp, talented people know other sharp, talented people who might fit what we're looking for. If you could give me two or three names of people just like you who you think would be interested in what we're doing, who would they be?"

Boom! Right there, you have their list started for them. It might even take them a minute or two to realize what you just did. You don't want to just make one or two phone calls. You want to make a bunch in a short period of time. Rapid fire action!

From there, continue the interview calmly and confidently. Walk them through each sequence to see if they are going to be a good fit, or if they meet our qualifications. You are educating the prospect while monitoring their interest level. It's a numbers game and the numbers are your friend—the more people you talk to, the more success you have.

This is a sequence, and if you can follow the sequence you are more likely to be successful with your interviews. If you can meet with a person face to face after a phone call, look sharp, sound smart, and follow the script, you'll attract quality people with a very brief meeting.

Another important step in the QI is to tell the prospect up front that if we don't have a good fit then we'll shut down our interview in 10-15 minutes and we're done. Let them know our opportunity may or may not be for them, and lower the pressure they might feel by assuring them, if they don't like what they see, it's no big deal. However, if the opportunity still makes sense to them after this short interview, you can go into more detail of what we do and what they can accomplish through National Agents Alliance. By setting the correct air of expectation, the candidate doesn't think you are there to sell them something. This type of mindset and posture does more to help set the tone than the actual words that you use during the chat.

As you're getting a feel for the interest level of the prospect you can ask additional questions like:

- Does this interest you at all?

- Do you think this is something that you would qualify for?

- Do you think you could satisfy our expectations once you got your license?

At this point in the face-to-face QI (or telephone QI), invite your prospect to an opportunity meeting. With about 50-60 of these meetings each week, you should be able to find one close to you, and the objective is to get the prospect in front of like-minded people and introduce them to our leaders. Our rotation meetings are definitely an important tool that you should be using.

The reason the QI is so important is because we want to get the plan in front of them two times—at least. The first time is during the QI in a more abbreviated, informal setting. This allows the candidate to process the information in a smaller, slower format. If they pass that first test, then they are qualified to come to an opportunity meeting. Then, when they attend an opportunity meeting they are able to see a much more detailed version of our opportunity and see the overall vision of NAA.

When a person sees the plan twice in a relatively short period of time, their comprehension level goes through the roof. If we don't do the QI and Opportunity Meeting in the proper sequence, the sheer volume of information presented at the Opportunity meeting may overwhelm the prospect. The first 20 minutes of the Opportunity Meeting could cause a mental lockup—like you just ran over their favorite dog—with the prospect staring at one of our leaders on stage with a dry erase board in an open room with a lot of people they don't know. It can be a little intimidating and even frustrating. They will be sitting there trying to figure out what is going on because you didn't conduct the QI first. Make sure you follow the steps!

REVIEWING THE QI IN THREE STEPS

With practice, you will become a good interviewer. When you learn to set the right mindset, posture, and control, you will be more at ease. You don't have to say a lot—sometimes less is better. Remember, you are the one interviewing. If your prospect is showing interest and you ramble on for 30-45 minutes, the posture is blown. Don't do that. It's the wrong approach. Just share the concepts in the sequence we've shown, ask more questions than you answer, maintain control, and speak in a calm, cool, confident manner.

Ask them this: "Aside from the obvious income levels, do any of the business development aspects intrigue you?"

It is a yes or a no.

It's important to understand that the person asking the questions is in control. Be mindful of the clock and do not run long. Even if things are going well, you do not want a 15-minute meeting turning into an hour. We have all heard horror stories about first dates that start off great but turn sour because one person put on the full-court press in the first quarter. Don't wear a person out the first time you have their attention.

Why would you want to do that anyway? Sharp business people can't afford to spend that much time for something they know nothing about. Give them just enough information to pique their interest and BAMFAM!

Keep things in sequence: the list, phone call, and QI should almost be bracketed together. It's one, two, and three. Learn to do those three quickly, and you'll be fine. If you can't bracket the first three basics in 24-48 hours, then you shouldn't even worry about the follow up.

THE FOLLOW-UP

We often call this "getting started." This is not a "checking to see if you are interested" situation. We've passed that point already. The follow up is about getting the new agent started and moving in the right direction. Is the prospect ready to do the next step or next 10 steps? It will be different with each prospect and you have to be the judge of what that person is ready to tackle. The key here is to just get the process started. Go in with the belief that the prospect wants to make money and is ready to move.

After the Opportunity Meeting, you want to talk to your recruit about what they just heard, introduce them to the speaker, and make the magic move of booking a follow up (BAMFAM) with them in the next 24 hours. Remember, every day you wait after a follow up without meeting again, you just diminish your probability of recruiting that person by 50 percent. If you can't do it in person, that's OK. You can do it by phone, even though it is preferred that you meet in person. If they are already licensed, you want to FasTract them, get them involved in the contracting process, train them on sales, and get them started. If they are not licensed, you want to get them enrolled in ExamFX. Above all things, because their interest in the first 24 hours is at its highest point, it is critical to access their warm-market list of names. The speakers should be covering this at the end of meetings, so your recruit should not be surprised when you bring up making a list. If there is an interest in building a team, let your prospect know they should put together that list now of at least 20-25 names, and get them to isolate the four or five people that stand out.

Some of your recruits will be only interested in personal sales. That's OK. If they have an interest in residual income, you need to set up a follow up and start working on their list. We want their 20-25 people and we want to identify the top four or five from that list. It is their assignment prior to the next meeting, same as the new agents who want to recruit, as well as sell.

For the recruit who does not have a license, get them to pull out a credit card and sign them up for a licensing class. Help them set a date to take the test, and put it on their calendar. That date should be no more than two weeks from the time they start taking the class. Your job is to provide the energy, the spark, the posture, and the motivation to get this new recruit going. By now, the prospect has given you indications that he/she is ready to go...let's move them forward!

Understand that this is huge on getting a new agent started. Your goal is to have width and depth, and you have a recruit chomping at the bit who is ready to start with NAA. This person has qualified as being open minded. You booked a QI and the recruit showed up, responded favorably, and is excited. The prospect then showed up at an opportunity meeting, which means he has given you three consecutive signals that he wants to get started with NAA. If you are tentative or hesitate on following up, you are going to lose. You have to go in thinking they are ready to go. If you were to break it down, the follow up is really 50 percent of the basics. If you are sitting on the mainland and there is an island out there that you want to reach, your bridge to that island is the follow up. The bridge provides a solid link between the initial contact from the mainland and getting to that island where you want to be.

Once the prospect has made a list they have the raw materials they need, and they are showing that they are serious about having a career with NAA. They passed their first assignment. When you meet with this agent, look over their list and let them know you're going to help them get started by talking to six to eight of the people on the list. You are going to help them find two or three people to start their team. Once you start interviewing with them in the field, their belief level is going to go sky high because their list is their highest-valued commodity, and they might forget that you told them you would only do a certain number of calls to potential prospects when you are really going to do as many as you possibly can. The idea is to maintain a lower number so they don't feel like they can monopolize hours upon hours of your time. If they think you are going to spend the next week working with them, the posture is gone and so is the urgency you worked so hard to create in the first place.

THE STEPS THAT LED YOU TO THE FOLLOW UP...

The list BAMFAMs to a call...the call BAMFAMs to a QI...the QI BAMFAMs to a meeting...the meeting BAMFAMs to a follow up meeting...a new recruit/prospect gets started! Do it again. Then, do it again!

UNDERSTAND THE TOP FOUR OR FIVE OBJECTIONS YOU WILL ENCOUNTER WITH FOLLOW UPS

THE NEW RECRUIT SAYS:

- "I only want to offer a small amount of time because of family, outside interests, etc."

- "I'm not ready at this time. I would like to start later."

- "I only want to be part-time. I don't know if I want to build something...sounds too hard!"

- "I looked online and I'm not sure I liked what I saw."

- "It looks like a MLM."

The follow up is not just a matter of finding out if they are interested and then moving on. There is a little more skill involved here. You BAMFAM them in 24-48 hours. Use their excitement. Get the recruit licensed, get them a new recruit, get them paid! These are the things that will overcome their objections. Take the recruit as far and as fast as they are willing to go. Find out where they are in life and then you will know where you need to take them. Get them to establish their reason "why" they want extra income, "why" they want their own business, "why" they want time freedom…all the objections go away. Obviously, what they are doing now is now satisfying their "why."

As you move a new recruit along, you end up back at the beginning where you start working the system with other people that you come in contact with. Follow the sequence. Do it all over again and keep building a bigger and bigger hierarchy!

Former presidential candidate and business mogul Ross Perot, along with others who made massive fortunes in the 1970s and 80s, liked to talk about people who have "skin in the game."

The phrase first appeared in publications around 1991, which means it was probably coined during the 1980s by Wall Street types. It's regularly been attributed to Perot and Warren Buffett. It sounds like a reference to bodily harm or something painful, but it's really just talking about a person who has a vested interest or has money on the line. They have a stake and it's an important stake to them.

The Oxford English Dictionary reveals that "skin" was used as a synonym for a "dollar" as early as 1930. Much earlier, a "skin" was a term used to describe a money purse in the late 18th century.

In our world, a person with "skin in the game" simply has a stake in something, or they are committed in terms of money, effort, and emotion. They have worked and invested in something and want it to thrive so that they get a return on their money, effort, and emotion.

In Buffett's world, having "skin in the game" referred to a situation in which high-ranking insiders used their own money to buy stock in the companies they ran.

The idea was—and is—to ensure that businesses and corporations are managed by like-minded individuals who share an interest in the company and its success.

"Executives can talk all they want," Buffett once said, "but the best vote of confidence is putting one's own money on the line just like outside investors."

Put your money where your mouth is! I like it. Regardless of who coined the term, "skin in the game" is about having a vested interest in something experiencing success.

If you were a teenager during the Vietnam War, then you probably were not 100 percent for it because you could have been drafted. If you drive hundreds of miles each week to work, then it's likely you think big oil companies are greedy and shouldn't be able to charge $4 for a gallon of gas. In both of those examples, a person's beliefs were slanted because they felt like they had "skin in the game" for various reasons.

When you have time, effort, and money invested in your business you can bet that you want to see it be successful or you wouldn't bother spending those efforts on helping it grow. The more you have invested in your business and in people, the more you want the business and your business partners to be prosperous.

By working with a new recruit on a list and helping get them started, you have "skin in the game," and you want them to know you are invested. Then, you want to help them get "skin in the game." Get them invested to a level that makes them want to get other recruits rolling. When you have "skin in the game" everything changes and your approach is different. Using the "Four Basics" is a great way to move a new agent to where they have enough invested in their own business that they will put forth whatever effort it takes to be successful.

HOW DO YOU KNOW YOU HAVE A SOLID PERSON THAT IS READY TO WORK WITH YOU?

Each of the prospects you work with have to be able to do three things.

- They have to be able to bring along their own width without your help—personally recruit.

- They have to be a team player—do the 8 Steps.

- They have to be able to take second and third legs— other than the tap root that you helped build with them—and take it a minimum of eight levels in depth.

When you get a recruit that does all three, you know you really have a person who has potential to be a leader. You have to help this person realize they need to bring their own width and take mentorship from you to take that second leg six to eight levels in depth the way you taught them with their first leg. If he/she isn't capable of doing what you are doing as you teach them, then all you have is a sitting duck or a frog stuck in the middle of a pond because it won't move. Until an agent builds the second and third legs, they haven't proven themselves. They can be a team player and recruiter, but, to be a real player in NAA, and deserve more of your time, they have to be able to take those second and third legs and build them.

WHEN WORKING WITH A PROSPECT, I GO IN THIS ORDER...

- Teach them to develop a list of names.
- Make recruiting calls for warm-market depth and cold-market recruiting.
- Teach them how to do TQI and QI.
- Train them how to do a One-on-One Meeting.
- Teach them to do a follow up and get a person started.

Training a recruit to do the first four things takes as much time as it takes to teach them how to do a proper follow up. You have to be a hands-on mentor to help a recruit build depth. You can't tell them how to do it and expect it to happen. A recruit has to prove they can handle objections and questions before letting them do follow ups alone. They can handle the first three things alone, but the in-person meetings I want to be in on. When doing the follow ups for a new agent in width, have them sit and listen to the objections and questions. They need to see the posture required for this and how to handle every potential situation that can—and will—come up during a follow up session.

How else can a person learn to do it unless they see it done properly? It's like a tandem jump when two people are sky diving. No sane person would expect a rookie jumper to leap out of a plane alone and reach the ground safely. You would have to be crazy to think like that! We don't want a recruit doing a follow up by themselves to start. The professional goes with the rookie, and they are on your back to make sure the jump goes safely.

TAP ROOT DIAGRAM

The worst thing you can tell somebody is that you are going to help build them a tap root, and then tell them to go hire in their width and sell without them seeing what you are doing to build for them. That's a great way to let a person get hurt. Take the recruit down the tap root with you, let them watch you work, so they understand what you are doing and they will duplicate what you are doing.

When we are working with an agent and we find a solid person in their depth who has a list of maybe 50 names, we move quickly. I get some of our top leaders that know what they are doing and blitz the list all out. It can get wild sometimes. There might be a dozen cell phones flying around a room and it probably looks like chaos, but it is organized chaos. We hit that list hard, and our cell phones get hot. It's not just one of us working the list. It's all our top people working phones, even though the person with the list gets all the credit. It's the power of teamwork!

One thing to be aware of is this: you work one leg—or two—for a recruit but not six. Doing more than that would be like putting a new recruit on welfare. A recruit needs help to get started, but it's up to you to make sure they can grow their team after you help with that first leg. The deeper you go in that first leg, the better chance you'll find another sharp person to work with.

It's been said quite often that "Chance favors the prepared mind." Prepare and go deep!

Why do you want to build depth? It's about stability and security. It keeps the pattern pure. It speeds up the incubation process to hatch that golden egg. When I'm building the tap root for a recruit, it makes them want to jump in and it speeds up their growth. They see it happening and realize that they want to do that too. They want to systemize things and the sorting process is magnified by running numbers. When I'm working depth, I can get a person to listen to me because they have something to lose. They've got "skin in the game" at that point. You want to help them grow to the point where they can't afford not to keep building and keep growing. It's indirect pressure, but it helps them realize they need to get out and produce. Even if they are only able to do $10,000 a month, it helps the volume.

When you have exhausted a warm-market list, then you want to help a recruit with cold-market calls after that. Don't stop warm until you have bottomed out in that leg. Then, you go with cold-market dials until you hit another recruit with a warm-market list and keep digging from there. You never know when a cold-call recruit will lead to a big, warm-market list.

DREAM DEVELOPMENT

"Champions expect to win.
They don't whine.
They don't complain.
They just win.
SHICKYBOOM!!!"

–Andy Albright

TALK
THE TALK

When I was growing up, I loved watching professional wrestling. Now, it's pretty much just World Wrestling Entertainment, but back then wrestling was really "rasslin.'" That's how we say it in the South.

Back in the day, you had all these different independent organizations like National Wrestling Alliance, World Wrestling Federation, American Wrestling Association, World Championship Wrestling, and so on. Those are all gone now, except for the WWE.

I remember when I was growing up, you had all these different outfits and all these crazy characters that were superstars. You had guys like Jimmy "Super Fly" Snuka, "Nature Boy" Ric Flair, Hulk Hogan, Wahoo McDaniel, and the Road Warriors to name a few. They were all bad dudes, and they could win over any redneck farm boy, make single women blush, and entertain crowds with the best of them.

> *"I'm a stylin', profilin', limousine-riding, jet-flying, kiss-stealing, wheelin'-n'-dealin' son of a gun! WOOO!"*
>
> –Ric Flair

These are a lot of names that most kids don't even recognize today. Young wrestling fans today will know names like John "You Can't See Me" Cena, Rey Mysterio Jr., Mike "the Miz" Mizanin, Randy Orton, and Triple H. These are the superstars now.

One thing that all those men have in common is that they are charismatic, athletic, driven workers that are among the best in the business.

I love the way they talk and I love the powerful image they project. They are a lot like the big-time coaches you see in the NCAA or the NFL. There is just something about them that sucks you in.

It was OK to be a quiet winner, but it was not OK to talk the talk and not win. It seemed like the wrestlers that talked the talk and walked the walk, by winning, had this dynamite element to them. When you put that combination together, it's awesome.

I was thinking about that when I ran across a story about Muhammad Ali, and how he thought he was confident in his abilities entering a boxing match until he heard the professional wrestler Gorgeous George Wagner, a champion in the 1940s, 50s, and early 60s, talking about an upcoming "bout" in Las Vegas many years ago. Ali, who was 19 at the time, was blown away by Wagner, who was then 46.

Ali and George were both on a radio show promoting their respective events. Ali was confident and told the host he was going to beat Duke Sabelong, a tall, big Hawaiian fighter at the time. Ali told them he was sure he would win, but it was spoken in a sort of "matter of fact" manner. Nothing over the top and nothing that would be considered controversial or headline news in today's world.

When Ali was finished, they turned to Wagner and asked him about his match. Wagner grabbed the microphone and started shouting, screaming, and bouncing around the studio like a mad man. He deemed himself to be the "greatest wrestler in the world." He was talking about tearing "Classy" Freddie Blassie's limbs off, "killing" the guy, and how he would cut off his own "beautiful blond" hair if he lost this match with Blassie.

Now, boxing's "Greatest Of All Time" is shocked. He cannot believe Wagner's antics. Ali was fired up to see this match just based on the "promo" Wagner just cut for the radio show. Well guess what? Ali did go see the match. The arena was packed. Thousands of people showed up to see Wagner—including the heavyweight champion of the world.

Want to guess what happened?

An arena of 15,000 watched Wagner beat Blassie. They showed

up to see Wagner get beat because he was talking. After the match, Wagner told Ali that people will always pay to see someone shut your mouth. He told Ali to keep bragging, keep on sassing, and to always be outrageous.

Ali admitted to people that he started boasting about his triumphs before fights thanks to Wagner, who was often referred to as "the man you love to hate." Ali took it to a higher level, when he started rhyming about what round he would "finish" off opponents.

It was not just Ali that had picked up on Wagner's genius. James Brown, the "Godfather of Soul" also admitted that he took notes and promoted his talents in music in the same manner that Wagner did with wrestling and Ali did with boxing. Brown wrote in his 2005 book, "I Feel Good: A Memoir in a Life of Soul" that Wagner helped "create the James Brown you see on stage."

Singer Bob Dylan also credited Wagner with changing his life. In his book "The Chronicles: Volume One," Dylan talked about meeting Wagner. "He winked and seemed to mouth the phrase, 'You're making it come alive.' I never forgot it. It was all the recognition and encouragement I would need for years."

Professional wrestling might not be real, but Wagner being credited with shaping the careers of three icons is!

From that point on, Ali's approach to things changed. He was never shy even when he was known as Cassius Clay growing up in Kentucky, before converting to Islam and changing his name. Ali started talking more. He talked a lot more. He talked so much that

> *"I figured that if I said it enough, I would convince the world that I really was the greatest."*
>
> **–Muhammad Ali**

fighters like George Foreman, Sonny Liston, Smokin' Joe Frazier and Ken Norton nicknamed Ali "The Louisville Lip."

Ali realized he had to do more than just fight. He had to talk the talk and walk the walk. He had a responsibility to make people want to watch him compete and fight. His interviews sparked debate and made people care about what happened in the ring. They would convince their friends to watch and take an interest. It was like starting a wild fire in a forest. The excitement would build and millions watched Ali and loved his persona.

These days it is called good "PR," but it was like nothing people had seen back then. Ali just called it "talking." By talking, Ali built an audience. Soon, Ali had built up a network of promoters, endorsement deals, and was a media darling/target. Whether you liked him or not, you knew what Ali was doing, and you knew when a big fight was coming up.

> *"I am the greatest, I said that even before I knew I was."*
>
> **–Muhammad Ali**

Ali was able to back up all the talk by performing, and that made his brand even more valuable.

Ali had an OK career. He won an Olympic gold medal for the United States in the 1960 Rome Olympics, became the heavyweight champion three times during a 56-5 career, and was named "Sportsman of the Century" by Sports Illustrated.

Now, back to the wrestling element.

My son is a teenager, and he—on occasion—will watch wrestling on television or go see a match when the WWE is in town. It's fun and it's a great entertainment.

My wife saw my son watching wrestling one day, and said, "Are you going to let him watch that junk?" I told her that I didn't think he would fall in love with it and go crazy, but I knew that he would learn how to talk the talk from watching wrestling. It is scary how he's learned to mimic that attitude, learned to talk crazy junk as a young man, and it is going to be fun to watch where he goes and what he will do. I do not think he is eyeing professional wrestling as a career, but I do think he learned from watching it. He learned that the WWE, like Ali and myself, we can talk the talk and walk the walk with the best of them.

If you are not excited about what you are doing, then it will be difficult to expect others to be fired up about things. If you have a meeting or event coming up, then you should be talking it up and getting others interested. Doing that is almost as important as backing it up with work. Take Wagner's example and imagine the impact it could have on another person. You might not influence the next Ali, Brown, or Dylan, but you could have a huge, positive impact on another person, and it could have a major impact on your business.

"To be the man, you've gotta beat the man!"

–Ric Flair

TOO BUSY
FOR YOUR DREAMS

People that aren't successful and aren't happy are guilty of finding every excuse in the world not to do what they really need to do to change that!

Life happens, and we are all guilty of finding time wasters and procrastination tools. It can be the Internet, ball games, TV, parties, social events, and so on. It doesn't matter why or what the excuse is, but we find a reason not to do what we should.

We waste hours. Hours turn into days lost. Days lost grow into weeks. Weeks spiral into months. Months become blink-of-an-eye years. We all know how fast years go by, and before you know it, you accomplished nothing.

The number one cause of failure in this business is lack of time.

You know the "I can't," "I don't have it," and "I wish I could" crowd that loves a good excuse?

They show up at the office and disappear for a few weeks. They start trying to get their license, but they never seem to finish. They want to go and set appointments and get into homes, but can only do it once, maybe twice. Maybe they even recruit a handful of people, but something pops up magically that prevents them from working with them. It's always something with a likes-to-make-excuses guy!

People are busy. I get that. I used to think I was busy when I worked in a factory, busting my tail off for somebody else's dreams. People have children. Children have needs. Life gets complicated quickly.

You've got the holidays, Father's Day, Valentine's Day, Thanksgiving, Christmas, and New Year's Eve. There's a barbeque for everything you can think of. You've got kids playing sports with championships at the city, county, state, and national level. You've got Final Four and Super Bowl parties.

What if we don't go? Will they come to our next party? That's the mindset I used to have and so many people have today.

Monday comes around, and next thing you know it's Monday again. You pay your bills and then a year passes and it's the same old, same old. Next thing you know you are 30 years old, then 40 years old, 75 years old, and the next thing you know you are gone. Life is faster than any of us even realize.

Everybody lived, but did you? A guy told me one time, "Some people figure it out and others just don't." Some people are living their life and other people are watching people live their lives.

I realized when I was watching the Travel Channel one day that I was watching other people. I figured out how to have time to watch while they figured out how to be there. They were there and I was watching. I was sick and tired of being sick and tired. I was sick and tired of watching other people live and me thinking about it. Me thinking that I didn't have any time to think about traveling.

I had to change my thinking and change what I was doing. I had to break the cycle I was in.

It's up to you to break that cycle too. You break that cycle because you know what is best for you and the people you care about. It's you that determines that, Bo! You want a better life, you want a better life for those around you, and you want the best for the people you care about.

Why in the world would you delay something important when it will pay off for you down the road—in both short-term and long-term ways?

Why wouldn't you work with a bright, sharp person that you have on your team, when it would help both of you? Why wouldn't you go "all in" to make sure your family gets to do all the things you never did growing up, that they get all the toys and cool stuff you never had when you were younger, and they experience life from a view that you didn't have until you opened your eyes and started chasing your dreams? How can you honestly say you are too busy for your own dreams?

Some people put in no time toward their dream, other people put in some time toward it, some put time in for a while and then they back off it. Then there are people that claim they do it all the time and they only work 40 hours a week toward their dream. Then, there's other people like pro athletes, people in the music industry, or artists that put their entire life into it. People that do put their whole life into it, I call them "all the timers" or "100 percenters."

The trick is to find people that want it. They want it so bad you can see it burning in their eyes, you can feel it when they talk with passion and commitment, you can witness it when they are "in the game" working with recruits and their clients. That's the person to spend time around. That's who you want on the team.

FIVE TYPES OF PEOPLE IN OUR BUSINESS

- No-time person (Too lazy to ever be good at anything)
- Sometimes person (Looking for a free ride)
- Part-time person (Afraid of commitment)
- Full-time person (Get by OK)
- All-the-time (A driven winner)

You can't do anything in life without time. The trick is that you do have the time. You have a lot of time. When is the best time? Right NOW!

Will you win 100 percent of the time? No! And nobody expects that. If you get a hit in every three at-bats in Major League Baseball, you are going to have a long, storied career. You might even make the hall of fame. Is that crazy? In a lot of things, it is. It's that effort and that drive that will separate the pack.

Can you make that effort? Are you willing to do the little things to get over the top?

If you worked on it right now, you'd be closer to being there than you ever will if you never get started. Move! It's like reading a book. If you just take 15 minutes and make that effort consistently, then you will finish that book before you know it. If you keep making that effort, that book isn't so daunting—like before you opened the cover. Let's say you are reading this book. Well, as you read this you are working toward your goal, working on your business, and taking the time to improve your business.

If you pick up a phone and call one of your upline managers once you put this book down to say hello, then they are going to give you some pointers. Talk to them about what you are doing and get some ideas from them. When you finish that call, you want to immediately call one of your new agents and see how they are doing. Give them some pointers you have learned from others. After that call, call a client and schedule a meeting to review a policy or their financial situation.

IMMEDIATELY do things. IMMEDIATELY, GO look at the Robb Report and pick out something nice that you would like to have one day. IMMEDIATELY, GO to the contest section of our company Web site, see what free trips you could win, and tell your family that you are going. IMMEDIATELY, print it out, put it on your refrigerator, and start working 24/7 toward that goal. At some exact moment in your life, every second starts to matter. Why not make that moment today that every second matters? Why not make it right now that you start working on your life now?

When will you start believing it can be different? Millions of people wake up, go to work at jobs they simply hate, and do things they don't believe in. How can somebody do that for 35-40 years? They can't stand the job, can't stand the boss, and can't stand the person jawing at them at the water cooler about something stupid that was

> *"No matter what business you're in, you can't run in place or someone will pass you by."*
>
> –Jimmy Valvano

on television last night. They do this over and over, week after week, month after month, and year after year.

Some of those people are great people. They love their families and their friends. They just don't get it.

In 2002, that's when I started. A decade later it was an overnight success. Nothing happens overnight, but everything happens overnight. Nothing happens in a second, but everything happens in a second. It's when you apply each second toward the goal where you start living the dream that it will be better than you ever thought it could be.

MAKING A DIFFERENCE

How can you change the lives of others when you haven't started by changing your own fortune? When you do this for yourself, it becomes easy to do it for others. My life and outlook changed when I made the decision that I was not going to that textile factory anymore. I'm not home all the time, but I bet that my wife and children will tell you they understand why. I'm chasing our dreams, "living life," and making a difference. It's not just for my family, but it's for other families too (Clients and agents alike).

No matter what your circumstances are, you will always be able to find somebody better off and somebody worse off than you. There's no reason for a pity party and there's no reason you can't work to be better. Why not help others in the process? Be a winner, be that person that makes a difference for others.

How can I make a difference?

- Decide to improve
- Be willing to "move"—do something
- See the system and its worth
- Work

THE
DREAM PLAN

The question is: how bad do you want it? For me, the "it" was to create freedom. It was freedom to have unlimited money, and unlimited time. The freedom to be on "my clock" and not another man's. I wanted the resources and time where I could travel the world with my family and friends. I desired the freedom that put me in charge of me with no restraints. Where are you? What do you want and how bad do you want it?

I sat in a coliseum one night with tears streamlining down my face as I thought about how bad I wanted freedom. The gentleman on stage described me being held under water and me wanting air so bad that I was willing to do anything to get it. As I pictured myself under the water, I started to scratch, claw and push, to tear at anything that would free me. I was willing to take it to the furthest extreme. You can let your imagination run wild. If I was on top of you with my arms around your shoulders and my legs wrapped around your torso holding on to you under water, what would you be willing to do? How bad would you want air? How sharp would you claw with your fingernails? How violent would you become to get that which you needed to thrive? Air.

> *"Get excited and enthusiastic about your own dream. This excitement is like a forest fire… you can smell it, taste it, and see it from a mile away."*
>
> –Dennis Waitley

As I pictured myself under water, I got the feeling that I needed to create my own freedom. I wanted to take that feeling that I had and put it in a jar so that when I was tempted to not work toward my dream, I would take out that jar and just smell that feeling…I would get that feeling back and all of a sudden my dedication would be through the roof. All of a sudden my focus would come back. I wanted to remember that feeling of wanting air, and I wanted to create that feeling in me of wanting to create freedom. That was my dream. My dream, as it starts to unfold, includes so many things for my family, and for my God. I wanted to donate incredible amounts to charities and causes I believed in (I am beginning to do that now in amounts that are staggering to me…more than I ever made). What are your dreams? What would you do?

> *"So many of our dreams at first seem impossible, then seem improbable, and then, when we summon the will, they soon seem inevitable."*
>
> –Christopher Reeve

I always wanted to be able to pick and choose cars like I wanted to. I wanted to drive them based on what they looked and how I liked them. It turns out that the very expensive cars do look the nicest and are the safest for my family. That's why I drive Cadillacs, Mercedes, and Range Rover vehicles. I wanted my income to continue to grow. My dream was huge then, and my dream is bigger now. I work on my dream every day by looking at magazines like the *Robb Report* and other travel opportunities available in this world. I look at car magazines. I go to car shows. I talk to people that are ten times wealthier than I am, and I imagine what it would be like. I'd like to buy a plane just like I buy a car. I would like to have a fleet of planes. I'd like to give a plane to a missionary.

What are your dreams? How bad do you want to get there? As

you think about what you want to have and do, consider this: There are three things that are very difficult to do: trying to kiss a girl who is leaning away from you, trying to climb a fence that is leaning toward you, and trying to help someone who does not want to be helped. I wanted to be helped and I desire to help people that want to be helped. I wanted to be respected by those I respect. I wanted people who have accomplished things in their life to respect me and accept me as one of their peers. I wanted to be able to afford to go where they go and hang out at the places where they hang out. Even today, I read and hear about super-stars, people that have accomplished things and, I think, "Man, what do I have to do to get there?" The question is: what dream is real for you? What dream do you have? What is your dream plan? Write it down, talk about it with those who can help you achieve it, and then, let's get after it. I wish for you the very best life has to offer, and I trust this book has been a launching pad and a starting point for your dream escape.

> *"Be a dreamer. If you don't know how to dream, you're dead."*
>
> **–Jimmy Valvano**

WHERE ARE YOU?
THE TRUTH

Be honest. Don't trick yourself, Bo. In Shakespeare's classic play, Hamlet, the king says to his son, "to thine own self be true." If you tell yourself that you've got plenty of money, and plenty of time right now, are you being "true to thine own self?" Is there something you would like that you can't afford? Can your wife really buy everything she wants? Do your children really go to the schools they want to go to? Do you really donate all the money you want to your favorite charities? Do you base decisions on the lack of or the abundance of money?

Honestly take a look at your finances. Is all your money based on your physical efforts? Do you have any residual income? Are your savings building up to the level you want them to? Do you love what you're doing at your current job or your current business? What would you have to do to make your current job something that you love and you enjoy and you want to do 24/7? If you decided to go into business, would you have the time away from your current business, or would you have to actually change jobs so you can have enough time to build your own business? Do you have a plan for your children? You need to be honest. What are you willing to do? What do you need to do? What do you need to let go of in order to build the life that you want? Can you continue to coach Little League? Or is that something that you just have to continue doing? If it is, continue coaching.

> *"He who is not courageous enough to take risks will accomplish nothing in life."*
>
> –Muhammad Ali

Do you always watch TV? Should you give up TV to build your dream life? What do you do, honestly, that is not something that is going to further your cause to create your dream life? The No. 1 person that you cannot fool is yourself. Once you're able to commit to paper where you are financially and where you are in life, you now need to sit down with your up-line, growing manager, a very profitable person in this business, who is in life where you want to be, and show them where you are now so that they can show you how to move on to the next step. If you will follow the proven system your manager lays out for you, your success

"All hard work brings a profit, but mere talk leads only to poverty."

–Proverbs 14:23 (NIV)

will surely follow. As stated in the next line from the Shakespeare quote from above, "and it must follow, as the night after day."

Just remember: be honest with yourself, be truthful.

NOTE: In reading this manual, I'm sure you've noticed that several ideas/concepts have been repeated throughout the book. This shows that NAA is truly a business of systematic duplication.

BEST OF THE ANDY BLOGS

The following is a collection of some of the best blogs I've written since my blog at www.AndyAlbright.com started on July 17, 2009. The concepts listed within have proven successful for me and others. I hope you enjoy reading these for the first time...or reading them again!

THE AUDACITY OF WHITE SHEETING...OR HOW TO USE A BLANK SHEET OF WHITE PAPER TO SOLVE PROBLEMS AND MAKE YOUR LIFE BETTER

You like that title don't you? Sucked you in and got you to read this.

Since you clicked on that catchy title, I'm going to share one of my secrets with you. After I tell you, you're going to think, "that's no secret" or "Andy is talking crazy again."

It's not really a secret, but it might as well be because not enough people do what I'm about to tell you to do.

It's not as much a secret as it is a method I use to help me deal with people, problems and planning. It's funny how things always sound better in threes and with the same letter for each of them.

I spend a lot of time in my office drawing things out with my "white sheeting" method. It works for me and it can work for you!

So, here's my advice. The next time you have a problem or know something is looming, go to your printer or your copier and pull out a standard 8.5 X 11 inch blank sheet of white paper. Next, you have to find a pen or whatever you like to write with. That's the easy part.

Here's where people get scared. You have to actually think and write down your thoughts and ideas. I know it's going to hurt your head to do this, but try it. It will get easier the more you do this. I do it every week. I've got white sheets at home, in my office and probably in my car. It's helped me so many times you wouldn't believe it.

Guys, do this every morning for a week and let me know if you get positive results from it. Leave me comments at the bottom of this blog. I want to know if it helps.

Write down what you are going to do that day, write what you are not going to do that day, three people you need to be around that day, and three people you will not waste your time on that day.

You can do this exercise for anything. I mean anything. I keep a stack of white sheets handy wherever I go because it's my favorite kind of paper to take notes on. When I can't find a white sheet, I call for Chris Reavis because he knows to have some with him just in case I want one.

Maybe you want to quit your job. Write down how you are going to do that. You might want to write down what you are going to do to make money if you are considering leaving that job too.

Want to be more productive? Write down ways you can do that. You know YOU better than anybody else and if you are writing down what to do it means more than if I tell you to do something or a friend tells you to do something.

You can do this with anything, ANYTHING, in the world. You are really just brainstorming on paper, but "white sheeting" sounds cooler. The act of actually writing it down makes it more powerful and it forces your brain to think, not somebody else's.

So, here's how you do the quit my job thing. Start with how many hours you work, how much you make an hour and what your expenses are. Look at the whole picture—good and bad. Do that and you've already got a white sheet going.

Do one on association. Write down three people that drain you or bring you down and explain how they do that. Write a note that says, "I will not meet, talk, or e-mail this person from now on!" You probably like this person, but they just don't add value to what you are working toward. It's OK to be their friend, just don't waste your VALUABLE time on them.

Now, think about three people you absolutely need to be around. Write down why you need to be around them and figure out a way to make it happen. Are they worth a drive, a call, or an e-mail?

If they are of high importance, you need to probably drive or fly to see them if they will meet with you.

Even if it takes money, time, effort, etc. you must get around these people because you think they will help you. That should be a high priority for you. Guys, it's a strategic approach. Find ways to cross paths with people as much as possible if you need to be around them. Get all the one-on-one time you can if at all possible.

If they like sports, take them to a ballgame. If you can't get face time, call them, write them, do whatever you can. Sometimes, it's going to involve spending money—maybe a lot of money—to get around certain people.

Just doing an association white sheet can improve your performance and get you in the right mindset.

Do a white sheet on time wasters while you are at it. Teach yourself how to ignore certain phone calls that you shouldn't take. Learn to disassociate from friends that aren't helping you be the best person you can be. Find people that will help you reach your potential.

Keep doing white sheets. Get a three-ring binder of them going and put it where you can reference it all the time. You might even want to name it something like the audacity of white sheets! Be creative.

Few people know to do what I just told you about, so I've just given you a secret that has helped me too many times to even count. I'm serious.

It's too simple to be good, right? Wrong!

IT WORKS!!! I do it every week and you should start doing it too.

Here's proof! Here's a copy of the actual "white sheet" for the birth of this book. Check it out!

OUTLINE FOR MILLIONAIRE MAKER MANUAL DIAGRAM

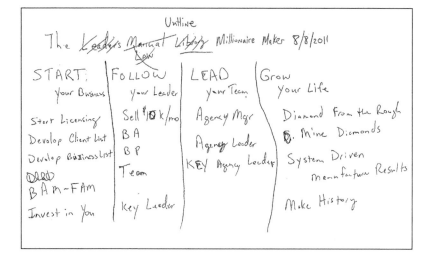

HOW IS THE NEW NOW!

People want to change and they want to change now, and I am getting ready to tell you HOW.

The way that you think determines the quality of your life. If you want to change something in your life or change the quality of your life, here's the most important question to ask: HOW?

HOW do I do it?

What you think about determines HOW you feel, HOW happy you are, and HOW motivated you are.

Can you say, "HOW do I do this?" "HOW do I do this?" and "HOW do I do this?"

In other words, the big subjects, like for example, HOW do I make more money? HOW do I have a better marriage? HOW do I get a promotion at work? Taking out a sheet of paper and writing down our "HOW" by coming up with answers to those questions changes your whole outlook on life. If we don't verbalize things and tell others about our "HOW," it won't happen.

Each one of us knows the answer to questions in our life. Questions like HOW to do great things, HOW to have great success, and HOW to find happiness, but if we don't put them on paper and verbalize as to HOW it's going to happen then it's unlikely that it will happen.

NOTICE WHEN YOU ASK QUESTIONS LIKE THESE:
- HOW do I become…?
- HOW do I get…?
- HOW do I feel…?

None of these questions relate to your history or have you looking back at your past. People that look forward as to what they are going to do or what they need to do and don't reflect on past problems, past mishaps and past miseries are the people who achieve. You past DOES NOT predict your future.

The HOW starts to create positive results because you are not looking back in your rearview mirror. You aren't going there—you're moving forward!

- HOW do I get this $400,000 car?
- HOW do I get that 10,000 square foot house?
- HOW do I get this promotion that is 10 percent more pay?
- HOW can I do something little today?
- HOW can I do something today that makes an impact on me? On others?
- HOW do I do it?

You start getting as tiny a "HOW" as you can get in the beginning. My suggestion is not to eliminate any small step, not eliminate any crazy idea. List all the possible ways that you can create this.

Robert Schuller wrote a book called "Power Thoughts" that deals with this subject. He talks about if "you are able to dream it, then you can do it." I love that thinking. It's talking about finding the HOW.

People that are more successful, people that are happier, people that do greater things in life are future oriented. People that don't live on past achievements or past failures create more. You want to be the person that lives and focuses in the future.

Don't sit around talking about what you did in high school like a lot of people do. You probably know guys that sit around and talk about playing high school football and HOW they almost won a conference championship. They remember every single play. They are just reliving their glory days even though it was 10 or 20 years ago.

You can't do that and keep moving forward.

HOW is the new NOW because you are not wondering if you can do something, and you are not saying maybe I can! You are focused on making it happen. Really, the only question is time.

We already know it's going to happen because we've talked about it, wrote it down, and we are focused on acting on those steps we need to execute to achieve something we want.

When you are focused on the future you are leading yourself with that dream and goal in mind. To lead anybody else, you must first learn to lead yourself.

To lead yourself, you write down the HOW and the HOW is what you are doing NOW to create your future. Doing that will help you design the life you want to live.

Go get yourself some NOW!

CREATING ATMOSPHERE WITH A PURPOSE

Atmosphere is created and there's nothing spontaneous about it. Think about it.

Here's an example. What's spontaneous about going around the bathtub and putting out rose petals, lighting candles, and dimming the lights? It's obviously being done intentionally.

Somebody created that environment for a reason.

You can create an atmosphere verbally, by waving your hands, making faces or even by just walking with a purpose. If I say, "hey let's go," and you start walking, then I've done it. You're curious about what I'm planning or where we are headed, but you are already following my lead. It's about having an attitude that creates an atmosphere.

Beyond that, you have to be aware that meetings have to be set up correctly to get the atmosphere right too. When it's not right then I get upset or even mad. You have to know what you are doing and how it will impact those in the room. You might have too many chairs or not enough. The lights might not be just right. There are lots of things to be aware of to get the desired atmosphere correct. You want to put people in the right frame of mind and create energy. If I'm closer to you PHYSICALLY then I can do that more effectively.

It's about creating the atmosphere.

People might say, "You did that on purpose didn't you?" Yeah!

You could say it's fake, but it's just like decorations at Christmas. People appreciate that effort and the atmosphere it creates. If you didn't have that tree all lit up and festive looking, then the room just wouldn't be the same, and the mood would be totally different.

That tree's creating atmosphere.

The right atmosphere can change a person's attitude. The right atmosphere can motivate a person. The right atmosphere can make all the difference in the world with your desired result and intentions.

Does that make sense?

Also, I love getting comments on my blog. If you have any questions, comments, or additional tips on this subject, please leave them at the bottom of this. I want to reach a level where any of my blog entries act as an ongoing dialogue for anybody that reads it. Any feedback, questions, or comments will help. I want to hear from you!

If you want to link this on your President's Club site, please don't hesitate. Help me share my teaching methods with others. Tell people to visit www.AndyAlbright.com and read my blogs!

Remember: Create atmosphere, make it like you want it, don't be embarrassed about it, and don't apologize for it.

Just do it and execute!

LEARNING AND COACHING—ONE LESSON AT A TIME

I want to talk just for a second about leadership and the impact it can have in our lives every single day!

It doesn't take much, just a little effort and interest in what's going on with people we encounter every single day. It can be powerful and it can be so impactful. In short, it can make a difference, but you have to make that effort! You've got to do it!

Here's what you got to do: You have to develop leaders!

When you read one or two pages out of a book on leadership, use it to grow your team. Grab somebody, sit them down, and relate your findings to what's going on with them and their work. It's non-stop talking. You will learn more when you teach that page or two, and they will appreciate it. You can't take an hour and a half; just take about 10 to 15 minutes. Do that all the time with people. Lunchtime…take a different person every week, take two people. Tell them, "Guys we're going to talk about one subject and we're going to hammer this one subject." You'd be surprised over a couple years how much you can pour into somebody.

Last thing today, John Maxwell comments that a biblical principle can do as much in a person's life as a biblical chapter and verse. The principle is Jesus, the principle is God. You realize that and it sets you free to talk to anybody!

SHICKYBOOMYOW!

ANDY, WHEN DID YOU GET CONSISTENT AND START WORKING HARD?

So I went to check my blog today and I saw that David O'Donnell down in Greenville, S.C., who works with National Agents Alliance and is one of our top producers and fastest growing agency managers, had been reading my blog, specifically the one I just wrote on "The Audacity of White Sheeting."

If you have not read the blog I'm referring to, go read it now. After that, come back and read this one so it all makes sense to you and you know what I'm talking about.

First of all, David didn't just read my blog, he engaged by leaving not only a comment, but he also asked a question—a great question!

Of course, questions get my brain going and I started thinking that I should select the best questions people leave on my blog and address them with shorter blogs. David, congratulations on reading and engaging! I like it, and I want to encourage you and the rest of the people that visit my website to continue to send me comments and questions.

Who knows, I might pick your question or comment and write about it!

Here's David's question: When did you start this positive habit and how long did it take you to discipline yourself to be consistent?

Now, David's question is not just about white sheeting, but it's more about a person's work ethic here. Does that make sense? See if you are disciplined enough to take the time to white sheet, then you are probably a person that is consistent in other avenues of life too. Successful people in business and in life are consistent. There's not really some big secret they know that others don't; they just know how to consistently do what they are good at. Here's another hint: they probably work hard too!

It takes practice and effort to get good at something. Those that know this, eventually become great!

It's like getting good at anything whether you are playing cards, playing basketball or running an Ironman race. You just start out doing all that you can.

David, I would remember to get out a sheet of white paper from time to time and just try it. I don't do it every day, every week or only on Tuesdays. I just do it. I do it as much as I can. I do it all the time. There's white sheets abound in my home, my office, my car, and everywhere.

My strategy has been for a long time now to do what I can do. I'm not big on setting limited goals, I'm not sitting on things that I've got to do, I just do all that I can do—all I can every day, all out. So, like I've been saying…it's all in, all year long! You've got to do one thing correctly, right now!

Then, you do another thing right tomorrow morning and another thing right for lunch. If you keep doing one thing right, it will start to mount up.

It fires me up when people ask me what they should do next. Start by moving, change your surroundings, do something you normally wouldn't do. Just keep working at different things and find out what you do well. White sheeting is one of those things I do that I've found to be an effective way to help me be productive.

Great question David! Keep them coming folks.

TIME IS $$$: WAYS TO INCREASE YOUR ROI

Return on investment: ROI. It's a term you hear all the time, typically in a business setting or when talking about finances. Your goal is to always maximize the return on money you invest.

When you mix your time with your ROI, then the game changes and the stakes are higher, much higher. Time should be thought of as your most valuable asset. Money is great, but your time is more valuable! Anything you do is an investment of time. You only get 24 hours in a day. There is no way to find more time. You can always find ways to earn more income.

If you enjoy going to sporting events, that's an investment. I like to watch the N.C. State Wolfpack and the Carolina Hurricanes. We invest money on tickets and when they play badly, I feel like I made a bad investment. It's also like I got a poor return on my time. Now, normally I take friends and family so it's not really a poor return because it's good, quality time we spend together, having fun.

If you break it down, there are many instances when your time is more valuable than money. Again, you can always make more cash, but time is something you just can't recover. Once a day is over, it's gone forever. When you treat your time as a commodity, and your actions as investments, it changes the way you approach your day.

How do we spend our time? We work, eat, sleep, exercise, socialize, etc…Each thing we do must be important or we wouldn't do them right? Of course! When we get out of balance and spend too much time in one area and not enough in others, we create or run into problems. Keeping the proper balance can make or break people that are trying to become successful in business, so it's key to find your correct balance. When we find that, we enjoy a productive and happy life.

How do we decide what we should be doing?

MULTIPLE BENEFITS

Does the activity produce more benefits for me than others? Will I get a positive return in more than one category by doing this?

If the answer is yes, you are getting a high ROI because you've multiplied your return and likely cut potential losses.

When I wake up to work out during the week, I normally have at least one person work out with me. I also keep my phone handy or read something that I can knock out during my workout. I've hit two areas by doing this. I'm getting exercise and I'm getting work-related items knocked out too. I'm setting up my day and how it will play out almost as soon as it starts.

Finding areas that intersect will help you accomplish more on a daily basis.

AVOIDING MULTIPLE SETBACKS

A negative can do so much harm that it can offset multiple positives or prevent future positives from even happening. Avoiding or minimizing these setbacks is as important as creating a positive. Engaging in activities that do not yield any benefit is dangerous. You've probably all seen a person that loves to go out drinking and carousing several nights a week. This person is spending time to do this, spending money on drinks and probably staying out—and up—way too late. They might not even have a good night after all of that. Now, they've got to wake up with a hangover and probably won't have a productive day at the office—if they even show up for work.

I'm all for people having a good time. Socializing is important and people should have fun, but that should not happen at the risk of several negative results. Often people get caught in a rut of repeating poor behavior and eventually it catches up to even the best of them. The more a person gets stuck in this pattern, the harder it is to break the cycle. To avoid this scenario, it's a great idea to evaluate what you are doing on a regular basis. I've talked about drawing things out in an earlier blog called, "The Audacity of White Sheeting" that I suggest that you read after you finish this blog.

YOU MIGHT ASK YOURSELF THE FOLLOWING QUESTIONS:

- Is what I'm doing a good investment?
- Is it time to make a change?
- Am I hanging around the right people?
- What can I do better with my time?

USING THE POWER OF COMPOUNDING

We've all heard about compounding interest. When you invest your money you earn interest on it. Over time, you start earning interest on the money you earned from interest. Years and years from now, this continues to compound and leads to a big pile of money! Shickyboom!

You can apply the same logic to your time. If you work hard when you are young, you are putting yourself in a position to enjoy success that will continue to add up for the rest of your life. Wasting time as a young adult just means you've lost time that you will never get back. Wasting those years cuts down on your ability to utilize the power of compounding.

When I was younger I didn't always make the most of my time. I finally started to realize I needed to take a different approach to things when I was about 35. Now, I always had a good work ethic and I loved to sell and trade things with people. Call it flawed logic or just not knowing any better, but I see so many people that never figure it out. They are more than contented to just do the silliest stuff and they are happy with their lives. I decided that I wanted more and I started chasing it. That's when my life changed drastically.

A lot of people don't value their own time when they aren't working, so they waste it doing things that have a poor return and doesn't help them solidify their future. Until YOU decide that your time is valuable, nobody else will either. If you seek a lifestyle that allows you to live like the classes (RICH PEOPLE), then you have to start making decisions based on what will yield a high return on your investment. That goes for your time, money, and emotion.

Your life is your corporation and you are the President, CEO, and employee. If you wanted something done now, what action would you take? If you wanted to make the most profit possible, what decision would you make?

Squirrel away some time each day—it will add up. Balance is the key.

Start thinking in those terms and see if you notice changes in your life and outlook. I hope this helps you and I'd love to hear feedback from some of you out there that try this.

Until next time, hammer down!

DELVE DEEPER

I think most people do not understand what to say when they talk to new agents on the phone, so they end up asking one sentence questions like, "How are you doing?" Then, they take whatever the agent says at face value.

They don't pry, they don't delve, they don't dive, they don't go deeper, and they don't peel the onion layers off. When you talk to an existing agent, you need to get to know their situation. You need to find out what's going on in their life.

So, the questions may start with, "How are you doing?" Then, you might ask, "Well, how many phone calls did you make?" You have to listen to what the agent is saying. If he says, "Well, I'm doing something with the children," then you ask, "How many children do you have? How old are they? Do they plan on going to college? Do you have plenty of money for them if something happens to you and your health?"

You are looking for the agent's "why." You are looking for the agent's "reason." You are looking for the agent's motivation. It is your job to turn that back around and ask, "Well then, don't you think you need to make some more phone calls right now?" So, you ask questions until the agent is doing what they need to be doing.

It's the same scenario with a client. You just don't take the client's word for it when he says he doesn't need any insurance. You start talking about his family, or what does his house look like? What does his dream home look like? What does his dream vacation look like? With an agent, you ask questions, and then you dive into getting the action that you need from the agent. You do the same thing with clients too. If you aren't getting what you want, then you see if you can speak to the spouse, you see if you can find out a parent's history, or if you can find out anything interesting about this new client/agent. You should make notes in your contact manager, in your notebook, in your thought notebook, or on a scrap sheet of paper. You need to find out what motivates this agent.

Eventually, you will be able to have one conversation with a new agent and that will be enough to understand them. You will always know what motivates that agent, and you can always bring that subject back to the forefront. You can put that subject back on the table. Then, you can say things like, "What happened to the people on the phone when you called them? Did you book the appointment? Why not?"

You can refer back to what fires up the agent, and you can encourage him to use that motivation when he is on the phone with other people. Once you find out a person's hot button or what motivates a person, you can use that to help that person succeed in life. That is why you spend more than just one or two minutes on the phone when you chat with a new agent!

STARTING WITH A GOOD STORY

So, have you been recruited by a manager that you don't feel like is giving you the information? In other words, you feel like a seed that's been planted in some non-fertile ground. You are a seed that is being kept out of the sunlight. You, as a new person, feel like you are not getting the information.

Well, first of all, your story is starting out wonderfully. Meaning, you can now tell new people that you hire, how rough it was when you were hired. How you used to walk uphill to school and then when you came back home, you had to walk uphill, too. You have a wonderful story that you can tell! So, you have a great start. See what I'm saying?

Sometimes we almost sound like the opposite. We're going like, "oh no, this is bad." No! This is good, because it makes for a great story!

If you were hired by a wonderful person, then you must succeed immediately. However, perhaps you have been hired into an organization that has not trained you properly; maybe your manager was too busy. Maybe you were hired by me, and you feel like I'm not telling you everything. Or, maybe your manager was sick and kind of out of commission when you got hired. For whatever reason, maybe you got a bad manager; it happens. Maybe you'll eventually quit. I'm not trying to be funny, I just don't know what your situation is, but you've got a good story because it started out tough.

What do you do now? Well, here's what you do. You find out as much information as you can. You be bold. You get no points, you get no bonuses, you get no extra credit for being shy or for being a scaredy-cat. You should come to the head office and ask questions. You knock on the door, ask to get in. You should ask to sit down with me. You ask for the information, okay?

At the same time, you sell a lot. The more you sell, the more people will pay attention to you at the home office. You plug into the conventions. You bring a tape recorder. You bring a camera. You sit in the front row. You ask questions. You be bold.

You go to my blog, www.andyalbright.com/blog, which you are at, obviously. You sign up, so that you get immediate information. You go to NAA Hot Spots. You go to those meetings, and you ask a million questions. You go to the web site. You read everything on the web site. You watch the videos. You go to my YouTube and you watch the videos. You learn my wife's name is Jane, my children's names are Haleigh and Spencer. You learn Alex Fitzgerald's wife's name is Heather. You learn everything you possibility can every minute of the day.

By the way, this is the way you succeed at anything. Even if the manager tells you everything, even if he's your coach and he's the most wonderful person alive, you still get the information for yourself as direct and as close to the origination of the source as you possibly can. That keeps it pure, so that he doesn't slightly tilt it, or slightly adjust it, or better yet, his interpretation of it.

So, now when you apply this and make some money, you will still have a good story of overcoming!

BUILDING A SALES TEAM DELIBERATELY AND SIMPLY (PART 1 OF 2)

Many times I hear experienced agents or experienced recruiters make a comment to their people like, "You must plug in, you must submit, you must use your upline…" and I want to walk up to this "experienced manager" and say, "What does that mean?!" If I am a new person, I do not know what you are talking about!

I want to explain to managers that they just need to get down to brass tacks, get down to the basics of what they want the people to do. So, for example, at an opportunity meeting, when you are asked to explain to a person or to the audience what they should do next, it should not be to "plug in" or "submit" or "use your upline manager." It should be things like:

- "You need to get your license and you need to complete that course."

- "You need to fill out contracting paperwork and get appointed with our carriers."

- "You should find out where the next event is and you should get signed up for that event. You should mark it in your calendar, and if you are already a licensed insurance agent, then you should get back with the person that you are chatting with at this opportunity meeting. Then, fill out paperwork and see if you can get appointed with our carriers. After that, you should come to the next event that we have scheduled."

I know these things sound like very basic simple things that anybody should know, but it is like gripping a golf club for the first time. You do not know whether the left hand is on top or the right hand is on top. You do not know if your hands should be together or three inches apart. It is the basics. It is like in basketball; if you have never played before, you do not know who gets the ball first. You do not know which side of the foul line you stand on. You know nothing! As a coach of new players, you do not just start talking big terms like it is time for tip off. You know you have to jump high in the tip off. No one new to the game would know what you are talking about! You have to speak in plain, simple, down to earth language. It is being deliberate and simple with the expectations or directions that a person needs to take next.

Do not make it so dramatic; it is SIMPLE—what we do! The ability to take the complex and break it down into the simplistic may be more amazing than to take something that is simple and make it complex. If it is complex, you do not get people duplicating the system. For people to duplicate you, you must be able to communicate deliberate and simple steps that anyone can follow. If you get one person copying you, you have doubled. If they get a person next week and you get a new person, you have doubled again. Now, you are four times bigger, with everyone repeating deliberate and simple steps, you have exponential growth, which is what you want!

Go get 'em!

BUILDING A SALES TEAM DELIBERATELY AND SIMPLY (PART 2 OF 2)

The goal is to break down the elements that a person needs to do into baby-steps or tiny bites.

You have heard the saying, "How do you eat an elephant? One bite at a time!" Well, if you can carve up the elephant in tiny, bite sized amounts and lay it out on a buffet to a new person, they can bite and eat, bite and eat, and eventually have the elephant eaten.

However, if you give a person a baby elephant to eat all at one time, you have created a feast and they don't know where to start. If you can chop it into tiny little pieces and they pick and choose what to eat real fast, you can rock and roll.

So, for example, if I am getting started with you, and you are not licensed, and you are a friend of mine, I might say, "Hey, do you have internet service?" See how quickly and how simply I broke that down? "Do you have Internet access? Go to the computer, sit down, log on, and go to www.nationalagentsaliance.com. Get your credit card out, sign up for licensing for life and health class."

Do you see how I am breaking it down into tiny bits of bites? Now, do not get me wrong, I am going to keep throwing more out there. I will tell you to make a list of people that you know that we might call, or I might say it like this, "I really need some help in Orlando, Florida, or Houston, Texas. Do you know someone out there that's pretty sharp? Do you know somebody that might want to make some money? How about somebody that might be interested that we can call?"

You see, I do not say things like, "Make me a list of people I might call for you," and don't try to make it sound like some glamorous thing. I try to make it so simple and dumb. No kidding, no joke. I can do that! Then, they just reach out and grab each of these bites. Maybe they say, "Great!" and they log in on the computer, and they name two people that they know in Houston, Texas. Or, they know two people that you should call, and now you are helping them take the bites of elephant. You are walking them through as fast as you can, and then when they get bogged down, that is your signal to go to talk to somebody else about baby snacks, about baby bites.

YOU might need to take baby bites or baby steps. Ask yourself, "What will I need to do next to get a new person that I can start feeding?" Maybe you need to brainstorm your list. Maybe you need to get out a sheet of paper and just start writing down sharp people that you have not called yet. Maybe you need to take a different look at it and say, "Okay, who do I give my money to? My banker, my insurance agent, my P&C agent." Since you are a life guy, you probably give money to a P&C agent. Start listing people you give money to: your realtor, your landlord, or the guy who does the utilities at your house. See, I am breaking it down in smaller bites rather than telling you go get another agent. I am trying to back up and even break it down for you.

The key is breaking it down in baby steps, but not taking forever to feed each bite to the baby. Lay it out on a buffet.

Hurry, let's go!

START WITH BABY STEPS

The first thing I would do if I personally hired you, would be to look at you and say, "Hey man, now that you've downloaded your software, go ahead and run a quote on yourself, then run a quote on your spouse, and run it on your kids." You should have them do it with different products.

For example, if I am starting a person off with Mutual of Omaha, and they've downloaded the software, I have them now run a quote on their mother, and then run one on their granddad. What happens is, our new agents start running those quotes, and they will say, "Oh my gosh, this software won't let you do an 82 year old!" They will start to learn the limits of the software, while they are running quotes.

Also, they will see the prices, and they will see how you can add on the riders, take off the riders, and other options that are available. The person starts to learn, and because they are practicing —doing the quotes on themselves—they are more interested in what they are doing.

Now I will say, "Ok, print off those quotes," and then I get with the agent and say, "Well, let's fill out an application on you, just so we can learn the process." We get all the way through it. We do the whole thing. The only thing left is for them to sign it, write a check, and they have bought (and sold) a policy. I got them right to the edge of the cliff on doing the right thing for their family, the right thing for themselves, and the right thing for their business.

If you are a recruiter, you are a salesperson, and you get a person that close, and you cannot close the deal and cannot get them to buy their own policy, either on themselves or on their children or on their wife, I'd have to look at you and say, "Seriously, you need to get with your manager, get with your growing upline, and chat with them about pushing people over their edge to do the right thing."

Did you hear what I said? Can you push people just over the edge to do the right thing for their family? Yeah, that will help them do some more personal buying, and that will help keep a lot of our brand new agents with National Agents Alliance, and eventually make a six-figure income, win all-expense paid trips just because they took those tiny little baby steps, and you pushed them to do the right thing!

FAMILY FIRST

I was looking over a survey we did recently of newer agents, and I noticed that a lot of new agents had difficulty selling their first policy.

When we start a new agent, it is VITAL that we get them off to a good start by selling ONE policy. Before you sell a THOUSAND policies, you have to sell one, first.

One of the best ways to do this is what I call: Family First.

Within a DAY of starting someone, sit down with them, face-to-face, and get them to do a list building exercise. This is basically where you use a prompting sheet to make them think of any and everybody they know. DON'T let them pre-qualify people. Just list names. Also, EVERYONE on their Facebook friends list should be on this list. If they are good enough to be a Facebook friend, they are good enough to buy insurance!

Now, the reason I call it Family First is because this list should now have everyone in their family on it. Call these people FIRST and set up an appointment to discuss their life insurance and annuity needs. EVERYONE should be able to sell a life insurance policy to at least ONE family member. If nothing else the family member should let them come practice their presentation on them, and you/they should tell the family member this. Go along with them if they are COMPLETELY inexperienced.

Now, this list can be used for policies OR for recruiting. A good idea is to make the appointment to go over their needs and bring up the recruiting while you are there.

NOW the EASIEST policy to sell for a new agent is one for THEMSELVES and/or their spouse and kids! Honestly, I do not have a lot of time for an agent that has not sold themselves a policy. I mean, what are you going to say to a client in their kitchen when they ask you whether or not YOU have a policy? If I ask you whether you have a policy or not, you had probably better LIE to me rather than to say you don't have one or whatever (Just kidding, don't write to me, I'm not telling you to lie! Just buy yourself a policy!).

The most important thing is to get some success for the new person and that comes with a SALE or a RECRUIT. Make sure YOU take a copy of their list. Sit there with them while they call, and in a few days, heck, YOU call.

JUST HELP THEM WIN!

WORKING FOR HIGH DOLLARS, VERSUS BEING YOUR AVERAGE GRUNT WORKER

OK, here is what gets me. You want to be the shortstop for the New York Yankees, but they have to work on Sundays. Listen to this, playoff games are played during the holidays. People want to be rich, but they don't understand what the rich do. Middle class is easy to get in. That's why it's such a big arena. Poor class is easy to get in, because somebody else will always tell you what time to show up.

Here is a quick rundown on the three scenarios. The poor class is the guy working at McDonald's during Christmas. Don't get me wrong, I'm glad McDonald's gives people jobs, but go to McDonald's during Christmas. They are actually open. That's typical poor class. Somebody tells them, you will work or you will not get paid. Middle class, that is the guy that takes more days off during the holidays because they're working and they're making $25/$50 an hour. They make "good money," so they deserve time off. Now look at the rich. The rich are on TV during the holiday season. They're sitting there playing football, and he's a quarterback, he's an offensive lineman and what is he doing? Not only is he working when nobody else is working, he's working through holidays.

So, you ask me, Andy, you want me to work all the time? No, I do not want people to work all the time. I want to be able to take a month off, a week every month off, but you've got to earn it. A lot of people say you need family time balance. I believe in balance, but balance needs to be coordinated with work. Where are you on achieving your goals? In other words, have you hit your goals and now you're there? You should take vacations. You should take off holidays. Every Christmas, Thanksgiving, whatever, Hanukkah, take it all off if you are where you desire to be. I'm going to tell you this: It is hard to maintain any level. So, are you sure you are where you need to be? Because it's going to drop a little bit if you don't keep the pressure on.

Now the poor guys. People tell them what to do, when to do it, or they're going to lose their job. Middle class, they've got a little bit of flexibility. They don't have to work at night. They don't have to work on holidays. They don't have to work on Sundays, they don't have to work on Saturdays. Okay, wonderful, wonderful. The rich, sometimes get unbalanced so that they can kill it. You hear about these shows, these TV shows that movie stars do where they're working 24 hours a day for three weeks straight. It does not matter what season it is. Even if it's your kid's birthday, during those three weeks you've got to be 24/7. Now, again, you say, "But they don't have a life." Some of them have a good life, a family life. Some of them figure it out. A lot of it has to do with what you want, but don't talk out of both sides of the mouth and say, I want it and then you're plugging along—let's say you're writing insurance and you're writing $5,000 a week. All of a sudden you take off two weeks in a row for Christmas when $5,000 a week barely paid your payments. Or maybe you're writing $2,000 a week and you are barely making all your payments and then you skip two weeks. When will you make it up? Everybody's always going to make it up on the backside. Then you find yourself in a hole trying to dig yourself out.

What I am saying is that you have to decide where you want to be and then WORK to get there. And it takes WORK to stay there. Is it worth it? ABSOLUTELY!!!

HELPING YOUR UPLINE MANAGER "WORK DEPTH" —USE COMMON SENSE

OK, so your upline is working down in your group, and he is a good guy, and your downline is a good guy. They're both good people saying the right things. You don't HAVE to be friends with this person in depth, but you DO need to coordinate with your upline that is working in your depth.

Let's say your upline is rather harsh in depth and tough on your person. Well, that's good, if they are teaching the right things. It's good, but let's say his personality rubs people a little bit wrong. There is nothing wrong with you being in depth talking to that same person, saying, "Hey Kyle, chill out. Chill out. I know David came in, and he's real hard on you, but he's hard on you for a reason. He's right about your persistency. He's right about your placement. He's right. And the goal is to win."

So don't let any personality conflicts get in the way of success, assuming there is a personality conflict.

Let's say that your upline, David, goes down in your depth and he's working hard, helping out. You can go up to your upline and say, "Hey man, you know my downline has good width, but he's got 17 other people he didn't tell you about. So Kyle didn't explain everything to you, David. He didn't share with you all the things that are going on. I don't think he's a great communicator. So just be aware, David, when you're in my depth, that Kyle is not a great communicator." So, even if your upline is working in your depth in your one big leg, you can still be in contact, setting the example and communicating with this person. It is critical that you coordinate with your upline, David in this example, and Kyle in depth, and make sure that you are intertwined. Make sure that you understand what is happening, and make sure that you pour gas on the fire, that you add to what's going on.

Now, let's say you are in the middle here, and David is working down in depth with Kyle, and you are a bad example: you skip convention, you don't write annuities, you don't follow the team player steps. Maybe you need to back away a little more, and let that person "take over" your depth until you are ready to come back strong. If you are doing the eight steps, and you are a great example, you should be involved, but keep in mind if it's your only leg, and your upline is working down in it, he has the power. He has the say so. He is "the man" because you haven't proven that you can have two tap roots, three tap roots, four tap roots, five tap roots. That is the point of our MVP. That's the point of our recognition. That's why we point out who has multiple, big, growing organizations, because that kind of proof is in the pudding. He's "been there done that," so we listen to him.

See, our culture is a culture of success, not a culture of should-be's, want-to-be's, might-be's. Ours is: he puts the puck in the net, he gets in the red zone and scores. Therefore, we let those people do the teaching. We don't get the losers, the mediocre people, the will-be's, and want-to-be's and should-be's. It's the people that did it. All right?

I hope that helps you a tad bit in depth.

WHAT IS 'DEPTH?' WHY DRIVE 'DEEP?'

In some companies they say 'drive depth.' They say 'depth is security.'

Here is the more traditional comment. "You need to network with the right people."

The deal is they are both the same comment.

The key to building a business is networking or driving depth with the correct directions.

For this article, depth will be the term used from here on out. The depth levels you drive down in need to be done with purpose and direction. The quality of your driving will determine the effectiveness of your efforts. Just like in driving to a vacation destination, if you make all the right turns you will get there faster, safer, and cheaper.

You get a quicker ROI and much better ROI for your family because you arrive at the destination quicker and start to enjoy your investment of time.

Here I want to start to provide improved decision making skills & directions for more effective driving depth. As always your ability to ask questions is the key to evaluating turns you make. To learn better question skills I suggest reading the book, *The Aladdin Factor*, by Jack Canfield and Mark Victor Hansen.

The next step is to learn to keep you antenna up and look for opportunity and know what you are looking for. It is NEVER a mistake to look for the sharpest three people one contact knows. An example is if you know an attorney, the question needs to eventually be; who is the sharpest attorney you know? If he gives you someone, then you know a sharper attorney according to his or her criteria. The key is to ask the right questions of the person you are dealing with.

STAY IN THE TRENCHES (PART 1 OF 2)

Just got off the phone with one of our agents and they were asking about how they can get one of their people to work with some of their downline. This is a common mistake people make.

YOU are responsible for your own depth!

You can't wait on your downline to work with people below them. You've got to get down there in the bottom of your organization and help the people get started correctly!

Any of your people can work on their own width. By HELPING them with their depth, you are securing your OWN depth, and locking everyone in above them. If your upline wants to get in your depth, by all means get out of their way, and don't forget to thank them!

All the top guys in our organization do this CONSISTENTLY! Building depth means building permanent, residual income, and everyone wins!

STAY IN THE TRENCHES (PART 2 OF 2)

The key here is: the upline person wanted me to TEACH them how to MAKE someone else do something! You see, the question they asked me was wrong. If I had even attempted to answer the wrong question, we would be condemned to failure! The question they should have asked is: "How do I get this organization moving?" Now the answer to THAT question, I can give! The answer is: Find a winner worth your time, and YOU go help them get 12 wide ASAP, and then you pick the best of those twelve people and YOU again help THAT person get wide!

You can't MAKE anyone do anything, but you can help a winner win!

YOU do the calls to friends, and YOU do the interviews!! YOU then help the NEWEST, deepest person get started. You teach, not on a conference call, but in person. The LEADER leads and YOU are one. Now go get you some people to lead!!

CONCLUSION

LOVE IS AUTOMATIC, RESPECT IS EARNED

A lot of people root for underdogs and paint consistent winners as villains, but one common theme prevails with a winner: RESPECT.

Why do people have a genuine respect for winners? Is it the aura they portray that attracts us to them? Is it that they lead a life few people ever get to taste, much less enjoy?

My take is that they combine things people love and hate. People embrace the obvious and reject that which they don't like. Winners do things most people don't...period.

Champions really do think differently. They expect to win. They don't expect to win in the face of weak competition or nonexistent challenges; they expect to win in the face of adversity, naysayers, competition, challenges, or energy vampires. They expect to win when they walk on the field, on a court, into a business meeting, and when they visit the homes of clients. They don't whine. They don't complain. They just win!!!

They do not let complaining hurt the team. They rise up above all the petty stuff that can be so damaging to a team or business. They impact the mentality of those they encounter every day. That positive mindset helps them compete at a high, successful level daily. They find solutions to any little hiccup that comes along.

Winners keep pressing forward, they keep moving toward the goal, and they don't let others cloud their vision and mission. They are optimistic because that gives them a competitive advantage over people that don't think positively. They add members to the team that share the same winning traits, values and outlook on the chase. They are hungry even when there is food on the table.

Winners know you can always push harder to do more, see more, and find bigger accomplishments.

Winners believe in themselves 100 percent. They bet on themselves daily. They believe that anything is possible. They set the bar high because their vision is on another plain. It's at a level that others don't even dare to dream. They want to go farther, higher, and do greater things than other people.

Winners finish strong in the last two minutes of the game. By the time the fourth quarter comes around, winners are almost running downhill. It's not an uphill climb for people like that, it is what they want. It's what they practice for and work so hard to get. They prepare for the moment when "the victory" is on the line. They step up and make a play that is the difference in winning and losing.

> *"Lazy people want much but get little, but those who work hard will prosper."*
>
> –Proverbs 13:4 (NLT)

Winners don't let "negative" clouds mess with the prize they seek. They take calculated steps to find greatness. Greatness isn't the house, the vacation, the car, or things like that. It's the work you do, it's the difference you make, and it's paying a price to reach the vision you have. Winners run when others walk. Winners hustle a little harder for a loose ball when others let the play end. Winners keep blocking until the whistle blows because they know it could spring a teammate free for a winning touchdown. They flat out do things differently than most people because they know there is so much more out there they can achieve.

Winners know that by not reaching their full potential, they are denying greatness, and they are denying the ability to help others strive for more too.

All the outside stuff doesn't matter to winners because they realize that distractions are the enemy of those who seek greatness. You can't be great when you are continuously hounded by distractions at home, work, and by other various activities. Distractions will prevent you from being great.

When you eliminate distractions, you start to have a laser-sharp focus when you go to work and you realize you can do great things. Once you reach that level, repeating this becomes important. Being able to repeat your successes makes you even better. When you can continue successful trends,you start winning—big time—all the time!

Winners make everyone around them better. They communicate better, they execute better, and they strive to be better themselves. Winners move faster, take action quickly, and do not wait on somebody else to create their momentum. Time is precious to winners because they know we cannot create more than 24 hours in a day. Once it is gone, it is lost forever. The next moment is always the most important to a winner.

Winners don't want to be like everybody else. They want to create a competitive environment where the team can thrive. Winners start strong and they finish strong. They do all the little things to prepare for the moment when all that work pays off. Winners embrace the fourth quarter!

Actor Will Smith says his secret to success is that he is, "…not afraid to die on a treadmill." Smith isn't afraid to outwork anybody. Being talented and smart, doesn't matter if you give up before the person that enjoys hard work. It won't work, if you don't work!

Winners are not bystanders; they want to be in the action mixing it up. Winners are the type of people who hear "you can't do that" and they set out to prove people wrong. They defy the odds.

Winners make a difference, they have fun doing it, and—listen up—they tend to make a lot of money in the process!

HAVING FUN
MAKING MONEY
MAKING A DIFFERENCE

Melanie Ray greets a dolphin during a vacation to Atlantis in 2011.

Here's a picture of me filming one of my live shows in my office with some of the NAA team.

NAA loves helping others. One of the many organizations we support is the Children's Miracle Network and Duke Children's Hospital.

Andy Albright and part of the NAA team traveled to Chicago to visit Chris Gardner in 2011 prior to him attending NAA's Leadership Conference in Raleigh, NC.

We love having fun at NAA, like when we had a 60s theme party on our SilverSea Cruise in 2011. Here we are with Mike and Michelle Alleman.

I mentor students at Western Alamance High School, where I went and my two children go to school now. I love helping young people and seeing their excitement for the future.

Andy Albright and Stormy hangin' out during a Carolina Hurricanes game.

The NAA team loves spending time together at events across the country. We've got a spot for you; want to join us?

The Goad family enjoys a swim with a dolphin in Atlantis during the summer of 2011.

NAA Whitewater rafting trip with President's Club Retreat in Charlotte on Sept. 23, 2011 at the U.S. National Whitewater Center.

Some of the NAA team joined Andy Albright in Seattle for a John C. Maxwell Exchange event in October 2011. Part of the trip including a tour of Microsoft.

NAA hosts Blood Drives for the American Red Cross annually at our corporate office in Burlington, North Carolina. It's just another small way that we try to make a difference in the world. Robbie Craft, Keith Hall, Katie Reavis and Missy Stipetich are shown after donating in this picture from 2010.

Some of the NAA team went to visit ExamFX's offices and took in a race in October of 2011.

Cortney Long, left, and Beth Katz, right, enjoy spending time associating with Jane Albright.

One of my passions is giving back to North Carolina State University, where I graduated from in 1986. I speak to Entrepreneurship Initiative students several times a year and serve on the EI Board of Advisors. Pictured with me, from left, are: Angela Hollen, an EI student; Jennifer Capps, associate director of the EI program; and Dr. Tom Miller, who is the executive director of the EI program. Proud to be part of the Wolfpack family. Go Pack!

The NAA team helped refurbish a school in St. Lucia during our SilverSea Cruise. The children at the Dame Pearlette Primary School were so happy to see us and were happy that we helped make their school better for them. Making a difference for people is what we love doing.

RESOURCES

www.NAALeads.com

- Our main website with information on our Opportunity, Profiles of Success, Testimonials, News and Media, a Sales Blog, and the all-important My NAA where agents find all the resources to run their business.

www.ShopatNAA.com

- Find lots of NAA apparel, office decor and great books to improve your selling skills.

www.NAA-TV.com

- Get the latest news about upcoming events here with our weekly "Did You Know" and "Rewind" videos, plus the regular Wednesday TV show.

www.NAAPresidentsClub.com

- Become a member of President's club and enjoy more association time with Andy Albright, have exclusive access to President's Club Night Owl Meetings and special trips just for our President's Club members

www.AndyAlbright.com

- Learn straight from the founder and CEO of National Agents Alliance through his blog posts.

www.NationalAgentsAlliance.com

- Keep up with the latest news from NAA here on their main blog page.

www.NAASupport.com

- NAA is here to support you all the way through your journey. If you have any questions, you can find the answers here.

www.NAAHotspots.com

- HotSpots are weekly opportunity and training meetings held in more than 50 cities across the country. These meetings help you recruit new agents by showing them what NAA can do for them.

www.NAALife.com

- Our lead-generating site. Clients learn the history of NAA and all the types of insurance protection available through our agents. There is also a link to job opportunities at NAA.

en.wikipedia.org/wiki/National_Agents_Alliance

- Learn about the founding of National Agents Alliance as well as other interesting history of our organization.

www.NAAUniversity.com

- National Agents Alliance provides NAA University as a starting point for those who seek to dominate in the field of insurance sales, and consequently live the lifestyle that successful people live.

www.LeadPerformanceTeam.com

- The Lead Performance Team handles all aspects of leads for National Agents Alliance. The LPT works with court researchers and Pro Data Research— NAA's sister company—in regards to retrieving data and distributing mailers to create the leads.

CARRIERS

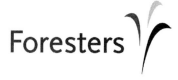

NAA BUILDING BLOCKS PACKAGE

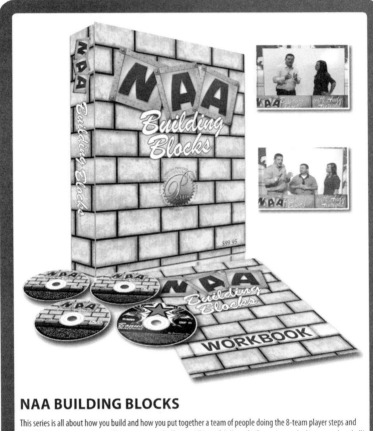

NAA BUILDING BLOCKS

This series is all about how you build and how you put together a team of people doing the 8-team player steps and the different ways you can toss them out to people. This is millions of dollars of information packed into one clamshell!

Featuring 30 videos, with literature, for growing your NAA business for long-term residual wealth from the master business builder, Andy Albright.

"You want to be a person who knows how to build. You need to be a person that knows how to put these blocks together. Everybody needs to have this! This IS your traveling university!" –Andy Albright

Includes 3 DVDs, workbook, and a bonus CD of materials to use when growing your business.

$99.95

NAA UNIVERSITY 100 PACKAGE

COACH   GINA HAWKS

NAA UNIVERSITY 100

NAA University™ is a training system for newly licensed NAA agents. A veritable crash-course in all things NAA, it is arguably the best new agent training system available for NAA agents at a 55-70% commission level. Plus, recent studies prove that new agents who complete NAA University submit more business, and get 31% more of it issued than those who do not complete the course.

Includes Study Books, 8 DVDs and MP3 discs, ExamFX discount code, online NAAU activation code, and much more!

$139.00

NAA Exclusive Books

THESE 3 NAA EXCLUSIVE BOOKS, ALONG WITH THE OTHER TITLES FOUND IN OUR STORE, WILL HELP YOU BECOME MORE OF AN EXPERT IN THIS FIELD. READING AND UTILIZING THE BOOKS THAT WE CARRY, WILL HELP YOU DEVELOP YOUR SKILLS, LEARN FROM OTHERS' EXPERIENCES AND MAKE MORE MONEY.

Eight Steps to Success
by Andy Albright
$24.95

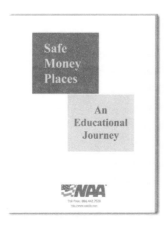

Safe Money Places
This 90 page simple read book teaches how banks, CDs, and annuities work. Increase your knowledge base to help you sell annuities and help families today!

$19.95

2012 NAActivity Tracker
$9.95

"ONE WAY TO BECOME AN EXPERT IN YOUR FIELD IS TO READ 100 BOOKS ON THE SUBJECT."

–BRIAN TRACY

A SPECIAL THANKS TO:

Mac Heffner, Becki Paskins, Jane Albright, Hal Wertich, Abigail Baumann, Barry Stephenson, Chris Reavis, Missy Stipetich, Kristen Crabtree, and the entire NAA nation for teaming up and allowing *Millionaire Maker Manual* to become a reality.

White sheeting at its best!!! My press secretary Mac Heffner took this picture one day at my house when we were working on the book you now hold in your hands. I hope you've enjoyed reading Millionaire Maker Manual!

"I firmly believe that any man's finest hour, the greatest fulfillment of all that he holds dear, is the moment when he has worked his heart out in a good cause and lies exhausted on the field of battle—victorious."

–Vince Lombardi